NO ROOM FOR GRACE

No Room for Grace

Pastoral Theology and Dehumanization
in the Global Economy

BARBARA RUMSCHEIDT

WIPF & STOCK · Eugene, Oregon

Wipf and Stock Publishers
199 W 8th Ave, Suite 3
Eugene, OR 97401

No Room for Grace
Pastoral Theology and Dehumanization in the Global Economy
By Rumscheidt, Barbara
Copyright©1998 by Rumscheidt, Barbara
ISBN 13: 978-1-61097-841-5
Publication date 12/1/2011
Previously published by Wm. B. Eerdmans, 1998

"This new edition is dedicated to the author's grand-children: Taylor, Sydney, Jordan, Sarah, Annie and Veronica"

Contents

CONTENTS

Preface

This book began as a Master of Theology thesis, *Living Between Fear and Hope: Doing Pastoral Theology as Winners and Losers in a Global Economy,* 1996. It emerges from a North American context of theological education for ministry. Questions addressed here come from my life in the United Church of Canada, a church with global partners, and from ecumenical experience as a student and teacher at Atlantic School of Theology.

No Room for Grace comes from a cumulative exploration of field education in community outreach agencies and its potential for nurturing critical faith. This involves a process of faith development/redevelopment that integrates structural analysis and theological reflection, through conscientization and spiritual discernment. I address particularly those who are committed to the ongoing mutual faith formation of Christians, in the local/global community of the church and in society at large.

Since beginning this study in 1994, I have become increasingly aware that pastoral relationships function within the social reality constructed by the "global economy." Pastoral ministry is affected by the ideological and spiritual context created by an economic system that produces surplus people. This structural phenomenon strikes at the heart of pastoral theology and calls for critical examination. It requires grounding in a rationale that is both personal/political and spiritual/theological. For me, within a local and global faith community of learners, such grounding has involved the embodied wisdom of particular persons.

Without teacher and colleague, Shelley Finson, I would have been unable to articulate my apprehension concerning the implications for pastoral ministry of an increasingly dehumanizing social context. She has provided permission, support, and guidance for pushing the boundaries of pastoral theology to accommodate such a critical hermeneutic. And without my life-partner, Martin Rumscheidt, I would have been without a particular experience of the concrete connection between conscientization and reconciliation. His critical awareness of dehumanization in Nazi Germany, his ability to learn and relearn, his access to cross-cultural contexts and global contacts have provided unending sources of insight, challenge, and inspiration. Shelley and Martin persist in making room for grace. Their unceasing help enables me to recognize how the personal is political and to name how the political is evangelical.

Introduction

The economic context of the late twentieth century is one of un-fettered capitalism on a world scale. Local, national, and continental economies have been restructured within an integrated free market system. The imperatives of "globalization" compel all members of the human family to secure their livelihood in competition against each other, in a global marketplace. A consolidation of this "global economy" has been proposed by the Multilateral Agreement on Investment (MAI), negotiated secretly in closed sessions around the planet, by the Organization for Economic Cooperation and Development (OECD). The alarming implications of MAI are grasped by science-fiction writer Spider Robinson, when he calls it a "planetary power-grab of unprecedented proportions."[1] In a critical response to this phenomenon he conveys the ethos of the OECD and the aggressive dynamics of "globalization":

> Perhaps the best thumbnail description I know of comes from my friend Michael Spencer: "If the MAI goes through, all the OECD countries combined will have only a few thousand citizens: the corporate investors. The rest of the hominid biomass will be converted to mere 'human resources.'"[2]

1. Spider Robinson, "The Scent of a Done Deal," *Toronto Globe and Mail* (Aug. 4, 1997).
2. Ibid.

INTRODUCTION

What does it mean to do pastoral theology in a world where people have been reduced to "human resources"? What happens to faith development when, subsumed within a mass of planetary resources, persons become the raw materials for competitive production and profitable investment? How are claims of Christian evangelism, e.g., "You are loved," or, "Jesus is Lord," nullified by the totalitarian presumptions of global financial marketing strategies? What are the pastoral and theological implications of the declaration by Renato Ruggiero, Director General of the World Trade Organization: "We are writing the constitution of a single global economy."[3] Can such claims be resisted in the name of God?

These questions come from analysis and reflection that relate economic realities to the dynamics of faith formation and the substance of meanings that matter. They address a faith dilemma that arises out of awareness and experience of the dehumanizing, exclusionary effects of the global economy. In such questions there is much at stake for the identity and mission of the Christian church. Given what the "hominid biomass" is asked to accept as reality, i.e., the way things must be, there is no room for alternate visions. Mestiza theologian, Elsa Tamez, from whom this book derives its title, sums up the situation unambiguously: "The law of exclusion that governs our context allows no room for grace."[4]

A critical relationship, both cognitive and spiritual, has always existed between the reality of dehumanization and the validity of Christian faith claims and commitments. Such tension is built into a faith tradition that was born, disseminated, and sustained in contexts of imperialism. There are echoes of this dilemma throughout Christian history. Voices from critical contexts in the past provide perspectives that reveal the credibility gap between the actual lives of actual people and Christian gospel promises. They can be heard as expressions of individual and collective faith

3. Maude Barlow, "Nowhere to Hide," *Canadian Forum* (April 1997): 9. For summary information on MAI, see Paul Hellyer, *The Evil Empire: Globalization's Darker Side* (Toronto: Chimo Media Limited, 1997), 4-6.
4. Elsa Tamez, *The Amnesty of Grace: Justification by Faith from a Latin American Perspective* (Nashville: Abingdon Press, 1993), 7.

responses, as concrete human experience of the reality of God in Jesus and the Christian story. When heard contextually, with an ear to the socioeconomic and spiritual milieu that conditioned them, these faithful responses provide invaluable resources of insight into how concrete faith is formed. Such critical dynamics can be identified in people(s) whose faith experience compels them to resist dehumanizing realities that contradict their understanding of the Christian gospel. A focus on critical faith responses, past and present, reveals both places of gracelessness, and evidence of the impossible possibility of making room for grace.

Readers of this book are invited to an exploration that is essentially one of critical faith development. The global reality of escalating dehumanization indicts any process of faith formation that denies, condones, minimizes, rationalizes, legitimizes, or is otherwise innocent or ignorant of mass human suffering. The specter of corporate capital acquiring legal power to preempt laws designed to protect the common good is ominous. It flies in the face of Christian belief in the goodness of creation, where humans are affirmed as cocreators, made in the image of God. Christian theologies become apostate if they foster acceptable powerlessness in the face of such idolatrous expropriations of God's creation.

A sense of the "global economy" as something scandalous may spring from a matrix of Christian consciousness, history, and pastoral tradition. Here "creation" is a word, not of science, economic necessity, or "virtual reality," but of faith. The emerging dilemma concerns creation as an article of Christian faith, understood and confessed not as incidental fact, but as covenant, as grace, as *new* creation. Such meanings are now being undermined or destroyed in the context of the global economy. This calls for concrete social analysis and theological reflection, involving a dialectical process of recovery and discovery of critical faith knowledge.

In a world dominated by the logic of the global economy, pastoral agency needs to engage Christians in a critical theological process of faith development as mutual empowerment. The task of assessing and addressing the need for such empowerment belongs to those who experience dis-grace, as economic exclusion and/or ideological and spiritual captivity. In this context, faith development becomes a project of affirmative action, for the task of actualizing our God-given humanness. This project may engage those of us who seek the liberation of all those "condemned not to choose for themselves a logic guided by the Spirit of life, which leads to justice and peace."[5] We need to integrate fear of dehumanization, overcome strategies of denial and evasion, expose counterfeits of well-being, and discover critical resources for authentic hope.

5. Ibid.

CHAPTER ONE

Dehumanization: An Issue for Theology and Faith

What Is Faith?

The Actual Faith of Actual People

Historian of religion Wilfred Cantwell Smith concludes that "fundamentally one has to do not with religions, but with religious persons."[1] Smith calls for a moratorium on the concept of religion in favor of the notion of the cumulative tradition, the story of the expressions of faith of religious persons, as the actual faith of actual persons. His articulation of this argument can ground operative assumptions about what faith is in terms of how it can be defined, developed, or redeveloped. Smith admits to not answering the query "What is faith?" beyond asserting that "the term refers to a personal quality of human life and history"; he aspires only to "a progressively more adequate and accurate answer as to what is and what has been, the particular faith of particular persons."[2] Wilfred Smith's claim to understanding is carefully qualified. It calls for an

---

1. Wilfred Cantwell Smith, *The Meaning and End of Religion* (Toronto: The New American Library of Canada Limited, 1962), 138.
2. Ibid., 170.

historical examination of the phenomenon of Christian faith. He provides rationale for approaching faith formation and nurture not as an appropriation or internalization of eternal verities, but as an ongoing process of human response to a human experience of God:

> If faith is personal, then even in principle it is not a generic entity, but a living quality. It is not a fixed something, but the throbbing actuality of a myriad of somethings. . . . In heaven there is God, seen by Christians as triune and active, known by them as loving. Neither for the outside observer not for the believer is there in heaven a generalized prototype of Christians' faith. Faith not only is but ought to be mundane, [a human] response. . . . The traditions evolve. . . . Faith varies. God endures.[3]

This concept of faith as having a dynamic capacity for growth and change can be illumined by Jaroslav Pelikan's important distinction between living faith and dead faith. Pelikan provides a warrant for faith development that nurtures critical consciousness and awareness of the connections between the human constructions of Christian history, tradition, and doctrine. He explains how such connections function, revealing their critical consequences for faith:

> Tradition without history has homogenized all the stages of development into one statically defined truth; history without tradition has produced a historicism that relativized the development of Christian doctrine in such a way as to make the distinction between authentic growth and cancerous aberration seem completely arbitrary. . . . The history of Christian doctrine is the most effective means available of exposing the artificial theories of continuity that have often assumed normative status in the churches, and at the same time it is an avenue into the authentic continuity of Christian believing, teaching and confessing. Tradition is the living faith of the dead; traditionalism is the dead faith of the living.[4]

3. Ibid., 170-73.
4. Jaroslav Pelikan, *The Christian Tradition*, 6 vols. (Chicago: University of Chicago Press, 1972), 1:9.

Faith Development Theory

In the light of Smith's working assumptions about religious faith, one need not start or conclude every exploration of faith development with a specific definition of faith. Direct and vicarious experience of both the assets and liabilities of religious faith may motivate an inquiry that looks for the origins of the redeeming and harmful effects of faith. How is the faith formed that determines what believers claim and do in terms of their Christian praxis, past and present? Given the outcomes of past faith formation and witness, what are the prospects for Christian existence in the future? Such questions may construe faith as a twofold phenomenon: as a human capacity that incorporates belief or mutual assent *(assensus)*, and as the basic orientation of the total person, a quality of trust *(fiducia)*, confidence, or loyalty.[5]

Understanding faith as having to do with meanings that matter means acknowledging social scientific theory that equates faith with individual meaning systems in general. Such theory includes the foundational work of James Fowler's description of faith development, and Lawrence Kohlberg's psychological theory of moral development. Their work provides resources for identifying discernible cognitive, moral stages that are characteristic of human nature everywhere. However, apprehending the redemptive knowing that informs and inspires particular, contextualized faith responses requires a different approach.

A grasp of what theology and faith can mean within the realities of the present world economy involves engaging macrosociological and metaethical factors such as globalization and dehumanization. This calls for analysis and reflection that can expose connections between what one believes and the privileges, constraints, and contradictions of one's material existence. Wilfred Smith's parameters for the study of religion suggest a process of critical listening, in this case, to faith testimony from those who are actual "winners" and/or "losers" in the context of the global economy.

It is liberating to think of faith, criteria of the truth of faith, and

---

5. Van A. Harvey, *A Handbook of Theological Terms* (New York: The Macmillan Company, 1964), 95.

the development/redevelopment of faith, not as abstractions, but as having to do with personal faith and the lives of real people. One can redirect the focus of faith development theory from generic growth and normative response patterns, to the response-ability of believers to particular life conditions, and to their contextualized faith dilemmas. More importantly, perhaps, distinctively Christian faith development priorities can shift away from a sole focus on reproducing "the traditional faith" as a given belief system, with absolute authority based on privileged insight into history and scripture. Wilfred Smith provides premises for exploring faith development as an ongoing, dialectical process of discernment and discovery.

> It is because the materials of a cumulative tradition serve each generation as the grounds of a transcendent faith that they persist . . . for the men and women who use them, they serve as windows through which they see a world beyond.[6]

His account of the faith that is in him shows that he lives his own life within these premises:

> There is no ideal faith that I ought to have. There is God whom I ought to see, and a neighbour whom I ought to love. These must suffice me; and my faith is my ability to see that they abundantly more than suffice.[7]

Globalization and Dehumanization

Dialectics of Cause and Effect

The term "globalization" designates a socially constructed economic process that has assumed the status of an economic necessity and an ideological imperative. In the following excerpt from a definition of "globalization," one can discern both what is posited as an objective meaning of the term, and the basis of the ideological and normative weight it has acquired:

6. Smith, *Meaning and End of Religion*, 144.
7. Ibid., 172.

4

globalization — The shift in investment, production, and trade decisions from serving national markets to serving world markets. With the continuing decline in trade barriers, the shift by most countries to market economies, the shrinking of communications and transportation time and costs, and the increasing rapidity with which technologies can be transferred, businesses now face competition from almost every part of the world. However, globalization significantly increases the pressure on companies to remain competitive and to develop specialized niches in the world market or develop alliances with the other companies to share the risks and rewards of the new economy. Globalization also increases the pressure on countries, through their economic policies, to keep their costs under control and to take into account the attitude of corporations, which can invest almost anywhere in the world, to new regulatory, tax, or social measures.[8]

Inasmuch as it impacts the social, political, and cultural context of the lives of people everywhere, the dehumanization inherent in the effects of globalization has material, spiritual, and ideological dimensions. If to "dehumanize" is to deprive of human character or attributes, then evidence of dehumanization can be found in the quantifiable facts concerning surplus or uprooted people(s), especially where they are already socially and economically marginalized. Dehumanization is masked in newly coined euphemisms: "casualties of progress," "yesterday's people," "the sacrifice ratio." It is discernible in the qualitative spirit of competitiveness that governs many interactions of ordinary life. In interpersonal, international, and intercontinental relationships, people are reduced to being either customers or products.

When examined in terms of their significance for theology and faith, in the context of the "global economy," "globalization" and dehumanization seem to be in a dialectical relationship. Is it the mechanisms and perceived necessities of "globalization" that dehumanize, or is this phenomenon made possible by the preexistence and availability of dehumanized people(s)? Assessing "globaliza-

8. David Crane, *The Canadian Dictionary of Business/Economics* (Toronto: Stoddart Publishing Company, 1993), 277.

tion" as cause, and dehumanization as effect, requires discerning consciousness. Giving epistemological privilege to critical voices from the past and from diverse contexts and conditions in the present can engender such consciousness.

Echoes of Critical Faith

In scriptures, doctrinal polemics, faith narratives, institutional statements, and official records, the Christian tradition reflects a continuum of cause and effect, crisis and response. The story often includes description and analysis that record personal and vicarious experience of dehumanization and scandalized faith. In our day we can access the voices of both victims and perpetrators of the "global economy," and of their predecessors and advocates, with the assurance that such documented experience is a vital source of meanings that matter. This repository of meanings can provide concrete resources for pastoral theologies that inform, question, and test Christian orthodoxy and orthopraxy. Such critical reflection promotes discerning consciousness with regard to the theological status and material condition of the created world and all those in it.

From persons and locations early and late in the Christian tradition, expressions of critical faith dynamics concerning creation can be found. For example, according to a proclamation attributed to Irenaeus (ca. 200), bishop of Lyons, "the glory of God is [humanity] fully alive." These words function as a theological articulation of critical faith. In this context they mark a polemical response to the perception of threat which many second-century Christians experienced in Gnosticism:

> The dangers that the early more orthodox Christians saw in Gnosticism were its pessimistic denial of the goodness of creation, its depreciation of bodily life, and its denial of the real humanity of Jesus.[9]

9. Harvey, *Theological Terms*, 105.

6

From the Russian branch of Eastern Orthodoxy, Huston Smith cites a saying that expresses a collective sense of critical faith consciousness: "One can be damned alone, but saved only with the others."[10] Here also, the words have contextual significance. They can be heard to function polemically, over and against Roman Catholic particularity. The saying proclaims distinctive communal identity and faith conviction through a view of the Church that Huston Smith finds "exceptionally corporate":

> Not only is the destiny of the individual bound up with the entire Church; it is responsible for helping to sanctify the entire world of nature and history. The welfare of everything in creation is affected to some degree by what each individual contributes or detracts from it. . . . In identifying the Church's teaching authority with Christian conscience as a whole — "the conscience of the people is the conscience of the Church" — Orthodoxy maintains that the Holy Spirit's truth enters the world diffused through the minds of Christians generally. . . . Individual Christians, laity as well as clergy, are cells in "the mind of Christ," which functions through them collectively.[11]

From lectures presented at Union Theological Seminary, New York, in 1983, Dorothee Sölle makes a faith claim and identifies hermeneutical criteria for understanding and valuing creation:

> We are made, created together. It is within our social existence that all the affirmations of the good creation are made, questioned, become true. . . . A genuine affirmation of God's good creation encompasses more than a tourist's perspective. To love God's good earth is to know about the hunger and exploitation of those who share the earth with us.[12]

In this hermeneutic, Sölle provides a critical tool for exploring a

---

10. Huston Smith, *The World's Religions* (San Francisco: Harper, 1991), 354.

11. Ibid.

12. Dorothee Sölle with Shirley A. Cloyes, *To Work and to Love: A Theology of Creation* (Philadelphia: Fortress Press, 1984), 30, 32.

phenomenon in which the "global economy" is experienced as a concrete contradiction to affirmations of the good creation. It renders such affirmations unbelievable, or utterly false. Integrating her earlier convictions, she writes in 1990:

> The biblical belief in creation considers three elements together: the creator God, human beings and the world. . . . The Christian understanding of creation is concerned to keep the creator God present, to understand created human beings as free and — perhaps the hardest thing to believe today — to regard the creation as good and to love it.[13]

Idolatry or Renewal of Anthropology?

Sölle's theological challenge foreshadows the critical faith dynamics inherent in another expression from contemporary Christian existence. It comes from John Pobee, who projects the shape of the dilemma that the "global economy" can present, especially for African Christians who claim to believe in and love creation. From the World Council of Churches (Geneva), in October 1994, Pobee proclaims, "We are, not because we are marketable, but because God affirms us."[14] He makes this polemical faith claim, over and against the proclamation of salvation by global competition. As an Anglican priest and staff member of the Unit on Unity and Renewal (WCC, Geneva), Pobee writes out of his own experience of the real life of real people in Ghana:

> Africa is not on the map because it does not seem to be a profitable market. Millions of youth and women are not on the map. Suffering today takes the dramatic form of exclusion. Exclusion is the ultimate expression of the death of the poor.[15]

---

13. Dorothee Sölle, *Thinking About God: An Introduction to Theology* (London: SCM Press, 1990), 43.
14. John Pobee, *Research Report 16: The Worship of the Free Market and the Death of the Poor* (Uppsala: Life and Peace Institute, 1994), 31.
15. Ibid.

In the political, social, and ideological context of the "global economy," individuals, communities, and peoples are not just economically exploited and socially marginalized. They can be and are in fact declared superfluous. The ethics of globalization is fueled by rhetoric that constructs a religious reality, where the market's right to life and freedom of movement supersedes that of human beings. As an African Christian, Pobee questions the growth ethic that pursues growth as an end in itself and reduces people to economic calculations:

> Under capitalism, there are no longer human beings with gifts, talents, and potential; there are only potential consumers. This reflects an anthropology lower than the biblical affirmation of humanity "in the image and likeness of God."[16]

In Pobee's identification of debased anthropology, one can discern a dialectical relationship. A critical connection exists between conventional forms of praising the glory of God, abstract affirmations of the goodness of creation, and concrete understandings of what it means to be human, fully alive:

> Where there is a positive anthropology, you cannot but respect people's interests. The question is what anthropology informs the economic and political activities in the international, multiracial, multi-cultural world community? That is a question to be addressed in the search for the well-being of the poor.
>
> It is important to take seriously the question of a renewed anthropology, not only for the sake of the poor, but also for the sake of the rich. People who peddle negative notions of other people soon imprison themselves with false images. They sooner or later destroy themselves.[17]

Rosemary Radford Ruether makes a similar point in identifying the critical faith dynamics involved in distinctively feminist understandings of authentic human nature (*imago dei*/Christ):

16. Ibid., 28.
17. Ibid., 31-32.

The uniqueness of feminist theology is not the critical principle, full humanity, but the fact that women claim this principle for themselves. Women name themselves as subjects of authentic and full humanity. . . . Defined as male humanity against or above women, as ruling-class humanity above servant classes, the *imago dei*/Christ paradigm becomes an instrument of sin rather than a disclosure of the divine and an instrument of grace. . . . Any principle of religion or society that marginalizes one group as less than fully human diminishes us all.[18]

John Pobee's call for a renewed anthropology conveys a sense of the competing faith dynamics at work in the "global economy," dynamics that manifest themselves with devastating concreteness in his African context:

The free market altar is that of privatisation where individuals compete with each other. . . . Ghana, which implemented both World Bank and IMF policies with the masochistic fervor of a reformed sinner, has seen no flood of investments as a reward. . . . The IMF gospel of "export more" is hocus pocus which misleads the search for viable economies. Competition among poor nations to export commodities, and substituting imported products for domestic, means a buyers' market, with producers of new materials at the mercy of buyers motivated by self-interest.[19]

Seeing the visible "death of the poor," by famine, disease, and genocidal warfare, gives Pobee new eyes. He now sees how the theological content and spiritual/moral integrity of Christian worship is challenged by free market idolatry. This critical perspective informs his theological rationale for economics and exposes what is at stake for Christian faith claims that affirm and call for love of creation:

18. Rosemary Radford Ruether, *Sexism and God-Talk: Toward a Feminist Theology* (Boston: Beacon Press, 1983), 19-20.
19. Pobee, *Worship of the Free Market*, 16, 17; see p. 26 for a holistic, contextualized understanding of well-being in the Akan (Ghana) word *ahoto* in what the Akan people define as "the seven graces."

When Christians talk about worship, they sooner or later talk about sacramental life. However, such a sacramental life is not just ritual or dogmas, or just a meal. It involves and is bound up with a dynamic, historical dimension. It is concerned with real change in social, economic and political life. . . . Using the word "worship" we dare not lose sight of the implied transformation of life, so that people and self may be in tune with the will of the Creator. . . . And precisely because economics should search for human well-being, it is, as well, a matter of faith, or a challenge to the belief in God, maker of heaven and earth. The well-being of all humanity, indeed of all creation, is the proper goal of economics.[20]

The Challenge of Critical Faith Development

"Compete and Be Saved"

Pastoral relationships that function within the social reality constructed by the "global economy" are conditioned by the ideological and spiritual context it creates. The good news of corporate capitalism proclaims salvation by global competition. But the bad news prevails in a contemporary global culture marked by violent death and spiritual death equivalents: fear, poverty, malnutrition, unemployment, addiction, depression, and despair. This dominant economic culture is hostile to the caring dynamics of human empathy. Its theology and ideology are aggressive: "look out for number one," "winner takes all," "survival of the fittest." Narcissistic spiritual formation and self-centered socialization are validated with monetary rewards. Awareness of and concern for the community of all creation becomes a personal, idiosyncratic liability, suspected by others as undermining a truly competitive social ethos. Faith development oriented toward personal and communal relationships of accountability and solidarity is displaced, discredited, and/or subverted.

20. Ibid., 8, 16.

11

Salvation Through Critical Partnerships

When making a living in the "global economy" is grounded in the anti-human logic of "making a killing," it may be construed as killing for a living. Experience of being held captive in a dehumanizing system of distorted social relations engenders a sense of impasse both within and outside the church. This raises questions for liberation and pastoral theologies, questions which demand personal, political, and professional integration.

A sense of urgency escalates in relationships of global partnership with Christians whose geopolitical and social location in the "global economy" is killing them. They name not only death-dealing economic structures (World Bank, International Monetary Fund), but also contradictions, illusions, and power imbalances functioning within the global Christian community. Such people can deliver critical insight and spiritual energy for the task of pushing beyond theological impasse. Catherine Ramokhele, Christian Council of Lesotho, and Omega Bula, All Africa Council of Churches, have identified concrete manifestations of unequal membership in the Body of Christ. In its mission magazine, Gawain Kenny reports to members of the United Church of Canada concerning a dialogue with these "partners in mission." The following perceptions of their and others' reflections on partnership between churches in the North and South show how dialogue between "winners" and "losers" can be mutually conscientizing and critically redeeming:

> It is premature to call ourselves partners in the midst of disparity and inequality. . . . Many observers and analysts of African political and economic affairs are saying that in the post–Cold War world, few seem to care about Africa. Despite the fact that many of its ills were caused or exacerbated by centuries of western interference and social and cultural destabilization, there seems to be little recognition of a moral responsibility on the part of the West to make reparations for injustices committed.
>
> How can we redeem partnership in the face of such imponderable disparity and callous disregard . . . and how should we view

the United Church which, despite its commitment to common mission is situated in a complex international economic system that creates and perpetuates global poverty and injustice?

. . . Mission today is truly global in scope . . . northern and southern countries are, to a large degree, suffering different manifestations of the same ailment — social and economic injustice that is global in scope. Ramokhele still would like to drop the term "partnership" [in favor of "friends" or "companions"]; Bula thought the term should be kept. Although it does not reflect the reality at present . . . "it gives us something to work towards together. . . . [If we] give up . . . because we realize we are unequal partners, then we will remain unequal partners. . . . We wouldn't be demonstrating a faith as people working together as Christians toward achieving equality. . . . Struggle, frank and open dialogue, sharing the good and the bad — these are the ingredients of meaningful partnership."[21]

Voices such as these can animate critical reflection on the "global economy" and the Christian tradition which has participated substantively in its growth and development. They call for a reinvestment of spirit in the critical conversion project of Christian pastoral agency and partnership. They provide concrete, living reminders that liberating, transforming resistance to socially constructed dehumanization *is* possible. Why are they so hard to hear? What blocks apprehension and comprehension of their message?

Banishing the Spirit of Inevitability

Conscious or subconscious experience of the "global economy," as both unredemptive and absolute, produces an escalating sense of inevitability. It contaminates the spiritual context of pastoral agency and undermines or nullifies faith claims that have traditionally underwritten Christian ministry. The symptoms of this spiritual malaise and its theological significance are aptly diagnosed by

21. Gawain Kenny, *Mandate* (July 1994): 22-25.

Dorothee Sölle and Shirley Cloyes as "theoretical theism and practical atheism:"

> "There's nothing we can do about it" is the voice of practical atheism. In the United States there exists a strange combination of theoretical theism and practical atheism. People believe in some supreme being "up there," but this heavenly being does not change anything here, neither in my heart, nor in my community, nor in the world.[22]

A phenomenon of "subliminal agnosticism" is observed by missiologist Jonathan Bonk, who makes a similar connection between cultural context and theological substance:

> The end result of an enculturation system in which God has been moved either to the periphery or off our cognitive maps altogether is subliminal agnosticism. The capacity to believe that God has actually and uniquely revealed [God]self through our Scriptures, that [God] has really entered human history in the person of [God's] Son, and that faith in [God] merits peace with God, has in many instances, atrophied, shrivelled or disappeared.[23]

For many Christians this kind of erosion of faith knowledge as inchoate theology reflects a loss of distinctive identity. This is recognized by ethicist Toinette Eugene in her call for a renewal of moral imagination as an antidote to despair. She appeals to the categories of Christian memory and identity:

> What is at stake here is: Who do we trust? Do we believe more in the chorus of naysayers who profess no radical (i.e., root) or ultimate belief in the God of life and peace, or do we trust God and God's gospel? The theological issue is Christological. The answers really do matter to the questions: Who do we say Jesus is? and Who does Jesus say that *we* are? . . . As James Baldwin wrote, "What they believe, as well as what they do and cause

22. Sölle and Cloyes, *To Work and to Love,* 72.
23. Jonathan Bonk, "Globalization and Mission Education," *Theological Education* 30 (Spring 1993): 52.

you to endure, does not testify to your inferiority but to their inhumanity and fear." Our identity is made at the places where we trust. Do we dare trust our identity with God, or with inhumanity?[24]

Capitulation on the part of many Christians to the cultural spirit of inevitability, in the face of a totalitarian economic system, is a function of underdeveloped faith and inadequate theology. The apparent readiness of self-styled believers to accept increasing levels of dehumanization as necessary, reveals a need for a critical theological process of unlearning, relearning, and new learning. What is called for is more than zealous efforts to bolster something already known as "the faith," and to apply it to economic conditions construed as "tough times." Redeveloping Christian faith that delivers redemptive knowing requires nurturing a recovery or a discovery of critical faith knowledge. The spirit of inevitability can only be banished by wisdom that knows — better than the market does — who human beings are and what we are created for. Motivation for engaging in a project of critical conversion involves more than a felt need for an alternative vision. It is inspired by the actual faith of actual people who, by the grace of God, have been enabled to know that dehumanization, though rampant, is not inevitable.

Dehumanization's Threat to Pastoral Theology

The Scope of Pastoral Theology

As an issue for Christian theology and faith, the dehumanization inherent in "globalization" presents a particular threat to pastoral theology. The challenge of this threat need not precipitate a categorical indictment of the tradition and practice of pastoral theology per se. Rather, it calls for an examination of the scope and mandate of pastoral theology and the adequacy of its resources for respond-

24. Toinette M. Eugene, "Globalization and Social Ethics: Claiming 'The World in My Eye'!," *Theological Education* 30 (Spring 1993): 24.

ing to a context of dehumanization. Such an examination needs to include critical reflection on "globalization," as a dehumanizing phenomenon that the Christian church, and its pastoral ministry, has neither caused nor prevented.

If Christian ministry is carried out in and for God's world, then pastoral theology may be understood as an ongoing critical activity that both informs, and is informed by, the church's practice of ministry and mission. Voices of persons engaged in Christian communities of accountability, e.g., Pobee, Eugene, and others cited here, testify that prophetic pastoral action in parish, congregation, and local community is becoming increasingly muted. The church's theological integrity, measured in terms of what it preaches and how it practices what it preaches, seems threatened by the impera-tives and concrete effects of the "global economy." Is this just a performance problem? a failure of contemporary pastoral theology to integrate Christian faith development, evangelism, and mission? Or, does it reflect a long tradition of diverse understandings of God, the church, the relationship of church and world, and the theolog-ical status of the world itself?

A clue to this query is the need felt by John Pobee, as someone "by training and occupation a theologian," to explain his "dab-bling" in economics. His rationale, excerpted here, proposes a working definition of theology. By implication, it expands the scope of pastoral theology to economic contingencies:

> Theology is not an irrelevance to economics and politics. For me it is the encounter with and experience of the human face of God in the contemporary world. Bread-and-butter issues (or, as other cultures would put it, the availability of rice and maize for all) are of the essence of theology and ethics. . . . [B]read-and-butter issues are as well religious and spiritual matters. This should occasion no surprise because at the heart of the Christian gospel is the incarnation. The prayer Jesus taught his disciples includes the petition, "Give us today our daily bread" (Matthew 6:11). Hunger then is at once an economic and a theological matter.[25]

25. Pobee, *Worship of the Free Market*, 5.

16

There are orientations to pastoral theology that involve discerning and articulating the "encounter" to which Pobee refers. Doing pastoral theology this way can mean expecting to meet God in human relationships, including unequal or unjust economic relationships. The following understandings provide a mandate for articulating that faith experience concretely and bringing one's findings to be tested in the community of faith.

First, pastoral theologian Larry Graham describes pastoral theology's collaborative potential for mediating, to the theological enterprise as a whole, the critical insights it derives from contextualized pastoral experience:

> Pastoral theology is defined as a subsystem within theology in general, and practical theology in particular. Its task is to develop theory and practice for the ministry of care. It draws resources for its creative work from the setting and act of ministry, the living tradition, cognate secular knowledge, and the personhood of the one carrying out the act of ministry. Methodologically, those resources are ordered by praxis. . . . Finally, pastoral theology, like practical theology, contributes not only to the formulation of theory and practice relevant to the ministry of care, but also recovers, corrects, and expands viewpoints in other branches of theology and ministry.[26]

Secondly, Homer Jernigan sees pastoral theology as an integrative activity with lines of accountability that are defined through its diverse yet mutually inclusive relationships:

> Pastoral theology is . . . dependent on all the other theological disciplines, . . . [it is] an integrative discipline that presupposes familiarity with all the other theological disciplines, . . . [it] helps the pastor "put it all together", . . . [it is] a relational discipline . . . [whose] primary concern is the quality of pastoral relationships with God, neighbor, self, and all of God's creation, . . . [it is] an inductive discipline that develops methods of reflection on

26. Larry Ken Graham, *Care of Persons, Care of World: A Psychosystems Approach to Pastoral Care and Counseling* (Nashville: Abingdon Press, 1992), 23-24.

human experience in order to inform, guide, and evaluate pastoral relationships. . . . Pastoral theology seeks to develop a transcultural perspective on human experience that respects particular cultural contexts but also transcends them . . . [and] communicates God's concern for persons in local, global, and cosmic situations.[27]

Doing Pastoral Theology in a Critical Context

Pastoral theology produces theoretical and practical resources for faith development. It can choose or avoid serving a dialogical ministry of mutual faith redevelopment, between economic "haves" and "have-nots," between victims and perpetrators of injustice. In a critical pastoral context where dehumanization is experienced and analyzed as such, Christians may relearn what humanization and rehumanization mean. This has to do with the epistemology of pastoral theology, how it learns and claims to know what it knows; about God, and about what violates God's creation. Graham's theological framework allows for hermeneutical and epistemological assumptions to be developed and tested in the context of ministry. This calls for critical consciousness and discernment. *Which* settings and acts of ministry are decisive and why? *Which* living tradition and *what* cognate secular knowledge is relevant? *What* particularities of the pastoral agent's personhood may symbolize blessing or curse in the actual lives of actual people?

Roger Haight's understanding of liberation theology as pastoral theology shows why and how, in an ongoing critical process, such theology recovers, corrects, and expands meanings that matter for all forms of ministry:

Like all theology, liberation theology may be defined as an attempt to understand God, ourselves, and our world in the terms of our Christian faith. What makes liberation theology distinctive lies in the particular experience and point of view

27. Homer Jernigan, "Teaching Pastoral Theology from a Global Perspective," *Theological Education* 30 (Spring 1993): 193.

from which this reflection on the faith occurs. Liberation theology depends on an experience of poverty . . . [and] makes sense only for one who has come into contact in one way or another with what makes up the lives of desperately poor people. . . . How does this [threefold] perception of the lives of poor people lead to a body of doctrine called a theology? The move can be explained in terms of the practical questions that face the pastor since the problem underlying the genesis of liberation theology is pastoral. How does the priest or minister tell groups of people that God is love when their whole experience of life is so negative? . . . One has to make sense of Christian doctrine in terms of people's lives.[28]

Writing in 1989, Haight compares liberation theology and the social gospel; he finds them to be similar responses to situations of poverty, social injustice, and oppression. He calls for a global consciousness which acknowledges the demographics of a Church which "is actually becoming less and less Western":

Once this perspective is opened, once the whole world becomes the horizon of the imagination, it cannot be closed again. . . . As human beings we share a common history — all of us are in existence together and in solidarity with each other. Christian theology, therefore, cannot find meaning for one sector of humanity in isolation from others. From this point of view, these two theologies suddenly take on a new and universal relevance for all Christians. . . . The meaningfulness of our whole history is called into question by the massive amount of humanly caused suffering and oppression we witness in today's world. No committed Christian, no religious person, can stand back and say that this has nothing to do with God and God's will, or God's providence, or sin, or the salvation mediated by Jesus, or the role of the church in the world. All theology today must become concrete and account for itself in addressing itself to the victims of the world.[29]

28. Roger Haight, "Liberation Theology and the Social Gospel," *Grail* 5 (1989): 46-47.
29. Ibid.

In the "common sense revolution"[30] of the late 1990s, to "reinterpret our faith in the light of our situation," on Haight's terms, means reckoning with an unavoidable and undeniable reality. The situation in question calls for the reconstituting of human lives as valuable — materially and symbolically. A reinterpretation of our faith must now be undertaken in the light of a "global economy" where neither the social gospel nor liberation theologies have prevailed against a Western culture's commonsense production of human surplus. Assuming this starting point precipitates the dilemma identified by André du Toit, in debates on The Truth Commission Bill in South Africa:

> Indeed all the issues involved in dealing with the past bristle with difficulties, and yet all of them seem important and urgent. . . . They present an overload of relevance.[31]

However, it is precisely in such troubled settings as South Africa that acts of ministry reveal Graham's "living tradition" to be what Pelikan understands as the "living faith of the dead." In the contextual analysis of many African Christians, e.g., critique of the World Bank's Structural Adjustment Programs, relevant cognate secular knowledge can be found. It can serve pastoral theology's task of developing theory and practice for the ministry of care in contexts dominated by a dehumanizing ideology. Especially evident is the particularity of the personhood of African women. They bring to their pastoral action generations of experience of race, class, and gender oppression. It is specifically in their faith response to economic crisis, that spiritual and cognitive insights are to be found. For example:

> We are burying our children everyday as if we were planting beans. (Edith Nawakwe, Zambia)

> You know, if a country is improving in economics or everything, it is the people who should be able to say. This policy outside

---

30. Slogan of the Ontario Progressive Conservative Party in its 1995 provincial election campaign.
31. Colin Leys, "Amnesty not Amnesia: Dealing With the Past in South Africa," *Southern Africa Report* 10 (May 1995): 32.

the country that says the country is improving — I do not agree. (Christine Ado, Ghana)

What is surrounding her makes her aware. If she goes to the hospital and there are no drugs, if she has to wait at the roadside for hours, waiting for transport, and there is no transport, much as she may not address it to the debt crisis, inevitably she's aware that things are bad. (Elizabeth O, Uganda)

If the liberalization that is being talked about really comes through, and is combined with concern for the human being as the ultimate goal of whatever you do, the future could be bright. This country has tremendous resources. It has got women who are really the backbone of the country. If they are given more chances, the future could be bright. . . . Change that saying by Jesus that man does not live by bread alone and say that a person does not live by spiritual things alone. Both bread and spirit need to go together. You need to keep body and soul together. (Gladys Mutukwa, Zambia)[32]

These are insights into both faith and economics that provide concrete resources for pastoral theology. It is the integration of what such women know, by both faith and daily struggle for personal, communal survival, that is productive of faith *content*. It is such critical content that can inform faith development and re-development between "winners" and "losers." Here are resources for recovery, correction, and expansion of both faith and *the* faith, in the sense of Pelikan's definition of Christian doctrine, as "the content of saving knowledge, derived from the word of God."[33]

This daunting task recalls Roger Haight's "pastoral" question. One needs to pose the question in accordance with one's own social location. For example: How does the priest or minister tell a group of people (or, how do we proclaim to each other) that God is love,

32. "To Be a Woman: African Women's Response to the Economic Crisis," Video Resource Guide (p. 9), produced by the Interchurch Coalition on Africa (Canada) for The All Africa Conference of Churches — Women's Desk, Nairobi, 1992. See Appendix 1.
33. Pelikan, *The Christian Tradition*, 1:2.

if and when we learn that the whole experience of life of so many of our human family tells them, and us, that they are being computed as economically worthless? Surely it begins with listening to the voices of those who refuse to be surplus, and then critically hearing our own responses.

It is not hard to find evidence that localized fear and globalized cynicism are hardening hearts and poisoning the environment for the real lives of real people. What are the prospects for believing in the glory of God as humans fully alive? The theology and faith that can negotiate the traffic between grace and dis-grace will need to begin with a critical reading of the context of dehumanization.

CHAPTER TWO

Reading the Context

Dehumanization

Apprehension and Comprehension of Harm

Reading the "global economy" as a dehumanizing social reality means both apprehending and comprehending harm in the economic process of "globalization." This process of inquiry evokes the dynamics, perspective, and vocation of pathology, focusing on death processes in the service of life and health. In the silent witness of a dead body, the pathologist seeks to apprehend or identify the cause of death. The task involves assessing the significance of data gathered, in order to comprehend or understand how and why the person died. Both etiological and forensic implications are involved in pathology's orientation toward the prevention of untimely death. This orientation is instructive for examining the facts of death in the context of "globalization," for apprehending causes of death and for comprehending such effects as inevitable or untimely.

The task of diagnosing deaths associated with the processes and conditions of the "global economy" can be construed as one of social pathology. A German feminist psychologist, Christina Thürmer-Rohr, has documented her experience of the psychosocial aftermath of the Chernobyl nuclear disaster. In her reaction to and reflection on this numbing, dehumanizing phenomenon, she provides some conceptual tools for analyzing and responding to dehumanization as symptomatic of a death process. She identifies "comprehension of harm," as a particular form of critical consciousness. It grounds and animates "productive hatred," as a loving, life-affirming response of resistance towards all death processes. Thürmer-Rohr's essay, entitled "The Prohibition of Hatred," is cited here to provide a sense of her critical use of these terms. First, the derivation and dynamics of "productive hatred" are articulated in the following excerpt:

> In 1972, Dorothee Sölle attempted to make the distinction between "blind" and "productive hatred. ". . . [To] blind hatred without hope Sölle counterposes "productive hatred," which she imbues with Christian social and political tradition. . . . Hatred in this case is a human capacity which results in being able to commit, to recognize, and to distinguish between justice and injustice. . . . Productive hatred . . . assumes identification with the victim and implies the struggle against injustice. . . . The way to dehumanization is not hatred, but de-emotionalization. . . . Just like love, [productive hatred] evinces a longing for transcendence, for surpassing what exists.[1]

Secondly, hatred as "productive hatred" is further explicated as a function of critical awareness; it is connected to and motivated by "comprehension of harm":

> Hatred, as it is meant here, is a category of *judgment*. It is not blind rage; rather it brings lucidity . . . requires reason as much as passionate feeling for the sake of continuity and reliability. It is an unconditional passion in the face of what should not be; it is the wish for the nullification, for the non-being, for the ought-not-to-be of what ought not to be, because it can be recognized as bad. It is a moral challenge to that patriarchal hygiene which acts to prevent the negation of those portions of the world which need negation by women. . . . This negation does not make "malignant creatures" of us, it does not make the person as a

1. Christina Thürmer-Rohr, *Vagabonding: Feminist Thinking Cut Loose* (Boston: Beacon Press, 1991), 177-78.

24

whole "negative." For the motive of negation is always the comprehension of harm: I want something not to exist and something else to exist; I want something not to exist so that something else can exist and not be harmed. This feeling, which can be called love — passionate arousal through the visualization — is not spectacular and does not seek strength and security; it sees the inconspicuous and finds value in what has never been noticed before.[2]

As tools of analysis for reading the context of "globalization" as dehumanization, apprehension and comprehension of harm contribute distinctive elements to a process of critical reconstruction of conscience, and faith redevelopment. Whereas apprehension of harm may arise from or instill fear, comprehension of harm can spring from hope, integrating fear as resistance.

A capacity for integrating apprehension and comprehension of harm in ways which are mutually empowering may be a key ingredient of critical faith and/or redemptive knowing. An example of this can be recalled in the faith claim of John Pobee, in Ghana: "We are, not because we are marketable, but because God affirms us." Pobee's announcement bestows ontological value on all human beings as those whom God affirms. It also apprehends harm in the well-founded fear of human beings being reduced to their marketability. Such harm is comprehended in terms of his own experience of African people(s) being defined as unmarketable. Harm is recognized, named, and denounced as suffering that takes the dramatic form of exclusion.

Similarly, Australian investigative journalist John Pilger apprehends harm in a " 'communications revolution' that is leading us into an 'information society.' "[3] Pilger comprehends harm in terms of his own experience that "technology has made almost anything possible — except truth."[4] Such harm functions in media misrep-

2. Ibid., 189.
3. John Pilger, "The Lying Game," *Life and Peace Review* 9:1 (1995): 21-23; from an edited version of a keynote speech at the annual Media Peace Awards, New Zealand, November, 1994.
4. Ibid.

resentations of events such as the Gulf War, when the suffering of Iraqi children becomes exclusion, where "the news will 'normalise' their suffering by continuing to exclude them."[5]

Through the analyses, narratives, and reports of the "global economy's" excluded ones and their advocates, dimensions of dehumanization can be discerned. This is not just a matter of apprehending harm in the ongoing anti-human atrocities to which they testify. It also involves comprehending harm in the socially constructed reality whereby their effective exclusion has been normalized as inevitable. Comprehending this harm is not automatic. Through a cumulative process of critical awareness, the realization grows that an increasing level of erosion of human well-being has become accepted as simply unavoidable. Economics and the entitlements/disentitlements of certain classes and conditions of human beings are undergoing contractual redefinition. Through this process, the meaning of dehumanization as the deprivation of human characteristics or attributes becomes concrete.

For example, in January 1995, in a feature article of a Canadian newpaper, John Stackhouse critiques the World Bank and UNICEF for "counting poverty," for turning development data into a marketing tool and turning reports into "catalogues of poverty."[6] As the *Globe*'s "Development Issues Reporter" in New Delhi, Stackhouse commends Tony Beck, author of *The Experience of Poverty,* for showing how "the world's development elite has not only reduced the world's poor to a statistic but has defined that statistic." Stackhouse critiques this phenomenon, analyzing a disturbing pattern of technocratic objectification of human subjects. He provides concrete evidence of a structured escalation of economic deprivation on a global scale:

> Mr. Beck writes that . . . constructs of poverty tend to view "the poor as passive objects of state planning." Villagers are no longer asked if they are hungry. They are asked what food they eat, and the responses are plugged into a caloric formula that tells the

5. Ibid., 22.
6. John Stackhouse, "Putting a Head Count on Poverty," *The Globe and Mail* (January 14, 1995).

surveyor whether the respondent should be hungry. . . . Mr. Beck believes rural populations actually fear people in positions of power more than poverty itself. Despite many of the images put forward by aid agencies, most of these poor know how to get food and shelter, and how to teach their children the basics of rural life. The threats of police raping their daughters, of local authorities stealing their crops, of landlords demanding more money: these are the real grinds of rural life. "Powerlessness remains the most pressing of problems."

Perhaps one reason powerlessness does not appear in development surveys is that it's a tough sell. It's easy to show a picture of a girl out of school or a boy with polio. It's tougher to convey the meaning of a picture of a landlord in rural Pakistan sipping tea with his brother, the local member of Parliament.

Gradually, however, some development agencies are cutting to the root causes of poverty. In its 1995 State of the World's Children report, UNICEF points to "falling commodity prices, rising military spending, poor returns on investment, the debt crisis and structural adjustment programs" for cutting real incomes in much of the developing world in the past decade.[7]

What is really going on here, and what is at stake for human attributes in the "global economy"? It emerges from between the lines of news items such as these. The cumulative and *unquantifiable* cost of these negative effects of the "global economy," itemized by Stackhouse, is projected graphically in another newspaper's feature story, out of South America. From Paul Haven, on assignment in Colombia, the story deals ostensibly with the issue of child labor:

> Bent double and gasping for breath, Lisandro Vanegas emerges slowly from the mine shaft, a 65-kilogram sack of coal and mud strapped to his 12-year-old back. His 14-year-old brother, Luis Alberto, is still inside, helping their uncle clear mud from the mine walls by candlelight. Behind the mud is coal, the lifeblood and the curse of this community.
>
> The boys of Angelopolis . . . work with their fathers pulling

7. Ibid.

27

coal from small family mines for $5 a day. Many never go to
school. . . . UNICEF is financing programs aimed at eradicating
child mining in Colombia and Bolivia as well as in India and
Bangledesh. . . . Colombian mines are narrow, some not much
higher than a metre, making children the ideal size. With no
heavy machinery or animals to remove the coal, boys and men
do the brute work themselves. In Angelopolis, coal mining is
virtually the only industry. . . . Ecocarbon, the state coal mining
company, which overseas Colombia's private mines, has pledged
to end child mining in two years. The company has sent agents
to mining communities to warn parents that child labor is a crime,
punishable by fines. The law is rarely enforced. Cielo Toro, who
runs a government social centre in Angelopolis that enrolls child
miners in schools, said the community's chronic poverty is breaking down family structures. "In addition to child mining, there
is drug abuse, alcoholism, physical abuse, child prostitution and
malnutrition," she said. "We are fighting an uphill battle to
change things here but we are fighting. All 30 children at her
centre still work in the mines. "We don't expect to get all the
kids out of the mines, because they have to work to survive,"
Toro said. "But at least through our program they can become
more conscious that they are human beings."[8]

In an uncanny way, this child labor story incarnates a meaning
provided in a 1971 Oxford Dictionary for the term "dehumanize,"
i.e., "rehumanizing the dehumanized members of society." Here,
Haven's journalistic account conveys the larger meaning of the
awesome challenge of rehumanization, in the context of both the
fact and the spirit of the lives of Cielo and the "children of the
pits."

Haven's report also provides echoes of the dehumanizing effects of forces at work in the early stages of capital accumulation
in Europe, in which the origins of the "global economy" can be
found. These dynamics can be discerned in the following passage
about the origins of a Nova Scotia labor leader:

8. Paul Haven, "Children of the Pits," *Halifax Chronicle-Herald* (April 20,
1995).

28

> Forced through economic circumstances to enter the coal mine at Wishey, in the South Dumfrieshire coalfield, at the tender age of ten, McLachlan [James Bryson McLachlan, b. 1869 Ecclefechan, Scotland] had, like thousands of other child miners of his day, learned the price of coal, a price paid in blood and suffering — occupational hazards that countless generations of miners and their families had been forced to accept in the earning of their daily bread.[9]

Later in my book, I explore such history as entanglement between Christian mission and the economic imperialism of European states. That history may also help to explain why Western communication networks and news services that serve the global marketplace can print critical investigative reports like those of Stackhouse and Haven, without jeopardizing their own interests or those of their shareholders — and perhaps, without even unduly disturbing their readers.

Who's Listening/Who's Hearing?

In the context of the Christian Church, one can discern dynamics of the dehumanizing effects of the global economy. Referring to denominational and ecumenical activity and experience includes accessing findings of those with a specific mandate to monitor the human condition, informed by both critical consciousness and "Christian conscience."[10] The material cited here can be viewed as measuring, but not accounting for, the threshold of tolerance for negative critique of the "global economy" in the United Church of Canada. This is an ideologically and theologically diverse Christian community, with a spectrum of "winners" and "losers" who are both perpetrators and victims in the "global economy."

The preamble to a report submitted to the Thirty-fifth General Council of the United Church of Canada, August 1994, by the

---

9. John Mellor, *The Company Store: James Bryson McLachlan and the Cape Breton Coal Miners 1900-1925* (Toronto: Doubleday Canada Ltd., 1983), 16.

10. Use of this term is explicated in later chapters.

"Moderator's Task Group on Canada's Economic Crisis," introduces terms of reference for understanding a theological approach to economics:

> The Greek word, *oikos,* meaning "house," "household," has given itself to three words in the English language which are therefore, deeply bound to each other: *ecumenical, ecological, economic.* What this means for all the people whose languages share this root word in their three equivalent terms is that the whole world, human and non-human, in all its diversity, is understood to be one "house"; and that economics (the law or *nomos* of the *oikos*) is the wise ordering of the "house" for the benefit of all, down to the smallest micro-organism.[11]

Significant for a study of critical faith is the phenomenon of the report itself and its ambiguous reception. In *The United Church Observer,* July 1994, the "General Council Preview" was headlined, "A Test of Shared Purpose," with subheading, "No one issue dominates next month's General Council: But the quest for vision looms large." Under "Council Issues," the preview listed "Economic Justice," summarized as follows:

> Saying the church doesn't need any new policy statements, the moderator's task group on Canada's economic crisis instead offers a list of thirty-six suggestions, and a bibliography of materials for local congregations who want to get involved in justice work. The task group . . . is also asking commissioners to pass six resolutions on issues ranging from the international debt crisis to alternative investments.[12]

In the *Observer,* October 1994, the "General Council '94 Special Report" was headlined "Council of Consensus," with a subheading, "The thirty-fifth General Council in Fergus, Ont., was a businesslike

---

11. "An Invitation to Seed Planting," *Record of Proceedings: Thirty-fifth General Council of the United Church of Canada* (Toronto: United Church of Canada, 1994), 223. See Appendix 2.

12. "A Test of Shared Purpose," *The United Church Observer* (July 1994): 16.

affair, lacking the fireworks of Councils past: For many commissioners, that was just fine." Reference to the Task Group's report was limited to "And it [Council] did pass recommendations on justice throughout the world but with no visible discussion."[13]

The United Church's response to the "global economy" and its effect on Canada is by no means exhausted in the apparent nonevent of a committee report. However, it is the report's content and the tone of the preamble that is significant for the recovery and discovery of critical faith knowledge, of redemptive knowing. Lines from the preamble are highlighted here to note congruence, contradiction, or confusion between provocative content, the *Observer's* interpretive comments, and General Council's apparent reaction/nonreaction:

> We have not thought it necessary or desirable to write once again a full analysis of the radically unjust, death-bound world that has already been written many times before. The problem is not lack of analysis; the problem is a failure of will — which is to say, of imagination and faith. . . . Biblically, faith is active obedience to God who is justice-love; it is laboring for kin-dom, for the Godly reality that is under the dreadful appearances of a world that lives (dies) by its egocentric, holocaustic faith. Those who do nothing show, by their inertia, that they are without faith in God.
>
> So we have tried . . . merely to point to things . . . [and] to remind one another and the Church of what we all, already, know; to invite further reflection and witness on the part of all who read it; and above all to animate to deeds — which is to say, to live a life of faith.
>
> For those who would like a fuller description of the demonic world in which rich, powerful countries aggressively sell sophisticated armaments to poorer countries and factions so that they can slaughter one another, or squeeze them to death by debt or by construction of trading agreements that give all the advantage to the rich, or where powerful undemocratic centres of money

13. "Council of Consensus," *The United Church Observer* (October 1994): 13.

(transnational corporations, money markets, conservative think
tanks) deliberately create chronic unemployment as part of a
strategy of gain, and manipulate whole governments to attack
their own weakest citizens economically, we direct you to the
annotated bibliographies at the end of this report [Fifteen Church
Documents (1983-94) and Thirty-one General Documents,
books, etc. (1973-1994)] which show only the tiniest fragment
of the literature that makes the full case. Have a nice day.[14]

The need to critique these remarks in the context of both the
whole report and its presentation within the limits of a conciliar
ecclesial process is acknowledged. The questions pursued here are
only those that out of an overload of relevance, appear to have
particular relevance for discerning the dynamics of the dehumanizing effects of the "global economy." The report recognizes that
"the United Church of Canada, to whom we now offer our report,
is itself a most *diverse* body" [emphasis added]. It also assumes
that "the analysis of the radically unjust, death-bound world" and
its "ego-centric, holocaustic faith," is well-known and understood
in the denomination and, therefore, does not need repeating. Is
such a perception warranted, if it implies that a consensus exists
in terms of apprehension and/or comprehension of harm? Does
it allow for the possibility that "failure of will," and "imagination
and faith" — the assumed causes of paralysis — reflect a diversity
that can account for the perception of intransigence, lack of proactive deeds, etc.? Do these factors not indeed reflect a *lack* of
consensus, concerning both a cost/benefit analysis of the "economic crisis" and appropriate faith responses to it? For example,
is the "economic crisis" viewed here as harmful or harmless? I
believe that a hermeneutic for addressing such questions must be
sought in the Council's muted response to the Task Group's
report, compared to other reported initiatives and actions of this
"Council of Consensus."

Commissioners, and through them, the whole church, were
challenged to sample a "fragment" of available evidence for the

14. *Record of Proceedings*, 224.

indictment of a "demonic" world ("the world as it is now because we have chosen to see and act in it that way") and then to "have a nice day." The tone of this provocative invitation conveys a mix of anger born of comprehension of harm, and resignation learned perhaps through past consciousness-raising efforts and policy/ study initiatives. That the responses of Council's "co-missioners" and the *Observer* reporters are grounded in similarly mixed emotions, reflecting diverse personal and ideological/theological content, is a possible interpretation of the apparently minimal engagement.

What resources of faith and critical consciousness are needed for Christians in the "global economy" to engage each other? What redemptive knowing will enable us to question and to be questioned concerning our beliefs — that God is present, that human beings are free and that creation is good? With regard to actual situations, such as the one from the conciliar church context depicted above, one might indeed re-contextualize Roger Haight's pastoral question by asking: How does the priest or minister [church Task Group] tell groups of people that God is love [that the world is demonic] when their whole experience of life is so negative [positive]? These questions sharpen a sense that resources need to be sought from diverse others; they identify the *facts* of the lives of persons who benefit from or pay the costs of the "global economy"; they discern the false and authentic *spirits* that nourish both their fear and their hope. This is a theological activity that is concrete and communal. It requires will, imagination and faith, and mutual empowerment for personal and structural analysis.

Structural Hegemony and Ideological Captivity

Critical Voices

Experiential insights from a diversity of others can be gained by listening. From the recent past, within or outside the church, they speak of socioeconomic distortion and their sense of structural captivity.

33

Voice: Participants in the 1990 Inter-Church Coalition on Africa study/visit, reflecting on the economic crisis in East Africa

> Many have observed that the debt situation is in fact less a "disease" than it is a "symptom" of a global economic order that is dysfunctional, inequitable and unjust. Measured against the biblical-theological criteria of just relationships and solidarity, the following specific elements of the system need to be rejected: an economy based on the competition of possessive individuals, structures of dependency, uneven power in the IMF and World Bank, the lack of legal protection for the poor, and the undemocratic imposition of life-destroying measures by governments upon the people.[15]

Voice: Ten Days for World Development, a Canadian ecumenical coalition

> Globalization of national economies has restricted national governments' policy options for addressing the crisis in unemployment and poverty. The oppression and marginalization of vast numbers of people around the world prevents their full participation in economic, political, cultural and social life. This deepens social tension and threatens human security.[16]

Voice: Maude Barlow, community researcher/activist, voluntary chairperson of The Council of Canadians

> Canada is in the midst of elemental change. Our social security system is being dismantled. Lucrative new markets run publicly in the public interest, are being opened to corporate speculators. A major devolution of federal powers to the provinces is being seriously considered. If realized, the federal government will be powerless to enforce national standards, resulting in weaker health, safety and environmental legislation and destructive in-

15. "The Price of Debt. The Human Face of the Economic Crisis in Africa," Inter-Church Council on Africa (ICCAF), Canada, 1990.
16. Ten Days for World Development, *1995 Action Resource*.

terprovincial bidding wars. . . . In international affairs, Canada has become a leading proponent of global free trade. In the feverish rush for new business deals, social and environmental priorities have been abandoned. Human rights violations, child sweatshops and toxic dumpsites are the hidden costs of the Liberal global economy. . . .[17]

"The Lying Game"

The "global market" rhetoric promotes simultaneously a cult of infinite possibility and absolute necessity. Media propaganda plays a vital role in what John Pilger identifies as "the lying game."[18] Thought control is accomplished, not by oppressive dictatorship but by a species of Orwellian language which is now the currency of news:

> Buzz words like 'moderate', 'reform', 'market', 'freedom', 'democracy', feature every night on television, everyday in the newspapers. But what do they really mean? And what omissions do they cover?
> It's never news that so-called 'market reforms' are causing throughout the world, what one development expert has described, as an 'economic holocaust.' . . . During the 1980s the Third World sent to the West $220 billion more than was sent to them in any form. That certainly wasn't news. The 'free market' in the West is as sacred as communism used to be in Moscow — an ideology dressed up as economic necessity, beyond scrutiny.[19]

"Global economy" rhetoric functions religiously as well as ideologically, through policy documents, press releases, etc. of international financial agencies, e.g., the World Bank, International Monetary Fund and their national partners, and economic "think

---

17. Maude Barlow, "New Directions," *Canadian Perspectives* (Winter 1995): 4.
18. Pilger, "The Lying Game," 21.
19. Ibid., 22.

tanks," Bank of Canada, Fraser Institute, C. D. Howe Institute, etc. For example, John Mihevc, of the Inter-Church Coalition on Africa, identifies a "theology of sin" that he discerns in the World Bank's major documents on sub-Saharan Africa over the 1980s:

> The duality between the inefficient economies of Africa and the efficient economies of the industrialized countries is the central organizing feature. . . . The redemptive call, issued by the World Bank, exhorts Africa to leave behind its sinful past to embrace the virtues of the market through SAPS [Structural Adjustment Programs].[20]

Mihevc characterizes such rhetoric as "more akin to religious discourse, a fundamentalist one,"[21] than serious, objective economic analysis. In the following passage, similar "religious" dynamics are identified and described by Franz Hinkelammert:

> The market becomes the Holy of Holies! From this moment religious images have as their very essence the negation of human beings and of their possibility for survival. Religion becomes the form of social consciousness that characterizes a society in which persons have delegated decision making power over life and death to a commodity mechanism for whose results they have relinquished responsibility.[22]

The Market Knows Best

The "global economy" is no respecter of appeals to collective altruism: love of neighbor, support and nurture of the weak. It claims hegemonic authority to define both common sense and the common

20. John Mihevc, "World Bank Thrives on Blame-the-Victim Image of Africa," *FocusAfrica* (June-September 1994): 9.
21. John Mihevc develops this analysis in *The Market Tells Them So: The World Bank and Economic Fundamentalism in Africa* (Penang and Accra: Third World Network, 1995).
22. Franz Hinkelammert, *The Ideological Weapons of Death: A Theological Critique of Capitalism* (Maryknoll, New York: Orbis Books, 1986), xiv-xvii.

good. As a prevailing economic belief system, it demands effective apostasy from competing religious and spiritual allegiances or covenantal relationships. Financial success requires an ability to repress and/or unlearn old social values, to dismiss them as misguided or irrelevant luxuries. One must rationalize new norms as necessarily nonnegotiable.

In the present social context, "winners" in the "global economy" voluntarily accommodate social attitudes and behavior to whatever maintains a competitive advantage over others. The entrepreneurial ethos of a market-driven economy animates individuals, groups, and nations through motivational rhetoric characterized by tough-minded colloquialisms: smarten up, get real, grow up, get a life, go for it. These messages alter, distort, and deform understandings of human possibility and interpersonal accountability. In such a desensitizing social climate, one is compelled to adjust one's mind to what is narrowly defined as "change," and internalize all aspects of what is now proposed as "reality." Persons, communities, and nations who are unwilling to accept, or unable to cope with this one-dimensional imperative to compete at any price, are held responsible for whatever economic fate befalls them. The epistemology and bottom-line calculus of the global marketplace make hardening of the human heart an ideological necessity, a condition for economic and psychic survival. Because humanly constructed economic imperatives have so succeeded in capturing both hearts and minds, they need to be analyzed politically, psychologically, *and* theologically. For such a task I find the concept of "triage" to be an appropriate tool of analysis.

Triage and Hardened Hearts

Three Dimensions of Triage

Different discourses can be drawn upon to convey three dimensions of the concept and reality of triage. The first dimension identified is a critical perspective from the United States. It comes out of a geopolitical context where the power to define and determine economic realities for the whole world is assumed and exercised. In *Tikkun*, a magazine of Jewish critique of "politics, culture and society," Charles Derber writes:

"Triage" is a term initially used in military medicine for the decision to abandon terminally ill or horribly injured patients in order to save others whose treatment is less time-consuming or costly. It has been employed in a different sense by sociologists to mean the sacrifice or abandonment of the socially weakest sector of society — the definition that I propose here. Triaged populations are cast-offs, non-persons stripped of economic prospects and social status.

One can distinguish economic, political and cultural triage, all of which are now surfacing in the United States. Economic triage can be seen in the withdrawal of viable employment or liveable wages from the sectors of the labor force, creating surplus populations with no economic prospects. Cultural triage is manifest in intellectuals' embrace of ideologies that explicitly justify the abandonment or elimination of surplus populations. Political triage involves the explicit decision-making by government leaders to stop assisting — with money, housing, or other services — the abandoned groups.

In the name of personal responsibility, Gingrich's counter-revolution would destroy the entitlements [New Deal and Great Society legislation] of dependent populations. . . . Americans would survive only by taking responsibility for themselves; the shiftless and irresponsible would lose their life-support system and sink or swim on their own. . . .

The Gingrich revolution has gained momentum because it translates abstract philosophical individualism into a radical and concrete legislative agenda, symbolized by the Contract with America. The contract proposes to dismantle much of the federal government. Yet, it is not government downsizing per se, but the change in its "covenant" with the people, that turns the contract into a manifesto of triage. . . .

Instead of entitlements, the contract proposes programs with restricted spending caps. . . . This is explicit political triage, in which government, rather than ensuring the survival of the entire population, designates certain sectors of the population as undeserving of support.[23]

I find a second dimension of triage implicit in analysis of the fallout from trickle-down economics and other more draconian approaches to defining and addressing the perceived needs of humanity. The geopolitical context of this discourse is Africa, the victim of a "culture of hard triage" (defined by Derber as offering formal intellectual and moral legitimation of abandonment).[24] In *African Agenda,* Patrick Bond reports that because of racism, the "Bell Curve tolls for Africa."[25] The title of Bond's commentary signals his critical response to the research of Dr. Charles Murray, who argues in *The Bell Curve* that biologically rooted racial differences in intelligence explain increasing economic gaps between rich and poor. Bond accounts for the limits of Murray's conclusions as follows:

> Murray has no conception of the circumstances, either contemporary or historical, faced by people not of his own race, class, gender and nationality. Murray uses invalid and indefensible techniques to make the case that blacks are not as smart as whites.[26]

African Agenda is published monthly in Africa, "to give an African perspective on issues related to politics, development, gender and environment, basic needs and culture." In an article entitled "SAPS threaten child health," this perspective can be discerned in critical comment on the results of hard triage:

> In Tanzania, where there is an eighty-five percent immunisation coverage of children, Health Minister Zakia Meghji says preventable diseases are responsible for the deaths of at least 200,000 children every year. "We are doing what we can to save the

23. Charles Derber, "The Politics of Triage: The Contract with America's Surplus Population," *Tikkun* 10 (May/June 1995): 37-38.
24. Ibid., 42.
25. Patrick Bond, "Bell Curve Tolls for Africa," *African Agenda* 1:1 (1995): 33.
26. Ibid.

39

children from unnecessary deaths," says Meghji, whose ministry's annual vote has been slashed from fifteen percent of government expenditure in 1980 to just five percent in 1995.[27]

The substance of an editorial by the managing editor of *African Agenda* reveals a spiritually destructive dimension of triage. With reference to Tanzania's severely threatened tradition of hospitality towards African refugees, Yao Graham shows how triage, as a global culture, undermines or destroys people's culturally and spiritually conditioned response-ability:

> Only weeks after such noble utterances [World Summit for Social Development in Copenhagen, March 1995] were made (and one year after the start of the Rwandan genocide) it seems that the wider world will merely stand and stare once more as Burundi slides into chaos. The big powers are more concerned with using the UN as a truncheon against Iraq and Libya than with mobilising to save a small African nation from bloody disintegration. In Copenhagen, Sadako Ogata, UN High Commissioner for Refugees, prophetically warned that unless generous but poor countries of asylum such as Tanzania and Zaire (which received over two million Rwandan refugees last year) "are supported . . . not only is their own development likely to be jeopardised, but their ability to continue to receive refugees can be threatened." Tanzania's declaration that it cannot take the growing numbers now fleeing Burundi is a grim fulfilment of Ogata's warning. Tanzania has a strong tradition of hospitality towards refugees from other African Countries. . . . Its refusal to accept more because it simply has no more resources underlines the importance of providing additional resources for the realisation of the key elements of the Social Summit's final documents. . . . The Social Summit highlighted that the crisis of social development is not exclusively a problem of the South. However, Tanzania's situation represents a microcosm of social development in Africa and the factors impeding its progress. It is one of the most severely indebted low-income countries; years of social development have been

27. "SAPS Threaten Child Health," *African Agenda* 1:4 (1995): 24.

devastated by structural adjustment policies whose neo-liberal policy thrust has worsened living conditions for the majority. Whatever other factors may be at play, Tanzania's inability to host more refugees cannot be divorced from these attacks on social development.[28]

A third dimension of triage is explicitly identified in the discourse of a Jewish scholar in the United States. Richard Rubenstein identifies and analyzes historical precedents for triage. His analysis functions as a faith response to both apprehension and comprehension of harm in the escalating production of surplus people. It is in this historically interpreted meaning of triage that much is at stake for human prospects in the "global economy." For this reason, Rubenstein's articulation of this meaning is extensively quoted here. His work on precedents for triage is itself a precedent for identifying the legal production of surplus people, and denouncing it as dehumanization. To argue that the "global economy" renders people(s) surplus means showing how "globalization" produces this dehumanizing effect, and why faith resources for challenging it must be developed. Such critical analysis needs to acknowledge and integrate what Rubenstein has already revealed about the "age of triage."

The history of the publication of Rubenstein's critical work is cited below. It suggests that in the United States, progress toward "politics of triage," as described by Derber in 1995 (without reference to Rubenstein), has been aided and abetted by an uncritical public consciousness and dulled collective conscience. By contrast, the foreword of *The Age of Triage: Fear and Hope in an Overcrowded World*, first published in 1983, reflects critical awareness and a live conscience:

> This book is dominated by a single concern: the fate of tens of millions of human beings whose lives have been either lost or blighted because they were unable to find a viable role in the economy and society in which they were born. This book is also a continuation of my earlier work on the destruction of the

28. Yao Graham, "Answer the Refugees' Call," *African Agenda* 1:4 (1995): 5.

41

European Jews during World War II, as well as an attempt to comprehend that terrible event in a larger historical context. As such, it is the promised sequel to *The Cunning of History: Mass Death and the American Future* (1975).

My earliest work explored the theological significance of genocide. The current work explores the economic, social, and cultural forces at work in modern civilization that make for *both* unemployment and genocide. Lest it be thought that I have abandoned theology and turned exclusively to political and social analysis, I wish to state my conviction that no theological enterprise, that is, no consideration of the ultimate values that move men and women, can be adequate to its task if it ignores critical political and social theory, especially insofar as these modes of inquiry seek to comprehend the conditions under which [people] attempt to conduct their lives both individually and collectively. . . . Had it not been for William Styron's support of *The Cunning of History*, which was expressed both in his review in the *New York Review of Books* (June 29, 1978), and his discussion of the book in his novel *Sophie's Choice*, there would have been no sequel to *The Cunning of History*. Styron's review appeared three years after the book's publication. At that time, the book had been almost completely ignored and had sold less than 1,000 copies.[29]

William Styron's introduction to the 1978 paperback edition of *The Cunning of History* provides interpretive context for exploring what is involved in appropriating critical meanings. Such meanings may stun or stupify, disturb consciousness or offend faith in ways which cause persons to withhold responses of affirmation or of protest, and to silence or repress self-questioning. What Styron illumines in Rubenstein is a phenomenon whereby a pastoral agent may function as a prophetic messenger, heightening cognitive dissonance, rather than, as in the more accepted role of the pastor/theologian, seeking to reduce it. William Styron, author of *The Confessions of Nat Turner*, introduces Rubenstein's book within the critical framework of his cognitive/emotional response to it:

29. Richard L. Rubenstein, *The Age of Triage: Fear and Hope in an Overcrowded World* (Boston: Beacon Press, 1983), v-vi.

Few books possess the power to leave the reader with that feeling of awareness that we call a sense of revelation. . . . If slavery was the great historical nightmare of the eighteenth and nineteenth centuries in the Western world, it was slavery's continuation, in the horror we have come to call Auschwitz, which is the nightmare of our century. . . . As a concept, as an image, we shrink from it as from damnation itself. . . . Rubenstein . . . has set himself the admirable if painful task of anatomizing the reality within the nightmare while the dream is still fresh. . . . He is making us understand that the etiology of Auschwitz — to some a diabolical, perhaps freakish excrescence, which vanished from the face of the earth with the destruction of the crematoria in 1945 — is actually embedded deeply in a cultural tradition that stretches back to the Middle Passage from the coast of Africa, and beyond, to the enforced servitude in ancient Greece and Rome.

Rubenstein is saying that we ignore this linkage, and the existence of the sleeping virus in the bloodstream of civilization, at risk of our future. . . . I have found Rubenstein's study at its most illuminating when he is dealing with Auschwitz as a phenomenon that is an inevitable continuation not only of slave systems in Western society but of exploitive "wage-slave" tyrannies that have kept [people] in bondage throughout history. The ultimate slavery of total domination that found its apotheosis in Auschwitz required only modern techniques of bureaucratization to achieve itself. Rubenstein's gift has been to show how that impulse toward domination has been embedded in our past and how, far from being extinguished, it adumbrates all of our uncertain tomorrows. Although he is wise enough to offer no specific prophecy in his pessimistic but rigorously honest essay, he leaves this reader, at least, with the feeling that the possibility of the nightmare being reborn to jeopardize the future — or perhaps even to preclude a future — is very real.[30]

---

30. William Styron, Introduction, *The Cunning of History: The Holocaust and the American Future,* by Richard L. Rubenstein (New York: Harper and Row Publishers, 1978), vii-xiv.

Hardened Heart/Rational Mind

The opening chapter of *Age of Triage* provides a critical framework for grasping not only facts but their meaning, and for locating the source of the spirit of the "global economy" in what Rubenstein calls the "revolution of rationality." It also helps to explain why the hardness of heart demanded by the imperatives of the "global economy" is so easily learned. It reveals how and why it can be tolerated, with such relatively untroubled conscience. Such innocence can be found in self-confessed Christians in the dominant classes of countries in the North, as well as in the counterparts of their client states in the South. Some of Rubenstein's analytical framework is excerpted with emphasis here, to be pursued in later chapters:

> With unemployment rising to its highest levels since the great Depression in both the United States and Europe, it is once again painfully apparent that few problems confronting modern civilization have been as insidiously corrupting or as destructive of the common good as the phenomenon of mass surplus population. A surplus population is one that for any reason can find no viable role in the society in which it is domiciled. Because such people can expect none of the normal rewards of society, governments tend to regard them as potential sources of disorder and have often attempted to control them or remove them from the mainstream of society altogether.[31]

Rubenstein identifies a population explosion beginning in eighteenth-century Europe. He perceives in it the consequences of "the triumph of an attitude of value-neutral, calculating rationality as the predominant mode of problem-solving in practical affairs" and he cites a "Faustian ethic," i.e., "a sense of mastery over nature and things."[32] He notes the irony whereby people, through instrumental reason, acquire the ability to achieve surplus production but in so doing, "take the first step in making themselves superflu-

31. Rubenstein, *Age of Triage*, 1.
32. Ibid., 1-2.

ous."[33] Rubenstein demonstrates that this phenomenon did not escape the analysis of Hegel, a German philosopher of religion (1770-1832). This connection informs my exploration of the dynamics of heart and mind in the construction of faith knowledge and critical consciousness:

> Even before the publication of *Phenomenology of the Spirit,* [completed 1806] Hegel understood the connection between surplus goods and surplus people. Writing in 1803 about the evolving worldwide division of labor that was beginning to make it possible for factories in England to supply cheap manufacturing goods to people in Asia, Hegel observed: "It thus happens that a far-away operation often affects a whole class of people who have hitherto satisfied their needs through it [their own craftsmanship]; all of a sudden it [the distant manufacture of cheap goods] limits their work, makes it redundant and useless." . . . In 1820 he wrote that it was inherent in the nature of what he called civil society (bürgerliche Gesellschaft) . . . modern bourgeois society . . . to overproduce both goods and people. Foreseeing that this would lead to the growth of a class of economic outcasts — an underclass within the heart of society — he described this process in a passage that has an amazingly contemporary ring to it: "When the standard of living of a large mass of people falls below a subsistence level — a level regulated automatically as the one necessary for a member of the society — and when there is a consequent loss of the sense of right and wrong, of honesty and the self-respect which makes him insist on maintaining himself by his own work, the result is the creation of a rabble of paupers."[34]

Was Hegel a social visionary? Was he a hard-hearted rationalist? Does this apparent apprehension of a flawed social reality reflect cognitive dissonance? Is it born of conscious comprehension of harm? Or, does it reflect a sense that however deplorable, things are the way they should and/or must be; as God intended? These

33. Ibid., 3.
34. Ibid., 3-4.

45

questions acknowledge an overload of relevance that is historical, philosophical, and theological. It is the experience of a theological dilemma that is to be pursued here.

Theological Impasse

Reconstructing Common Sense

It seems that a theological impasse arises not before, but only after the experience of comprehension of harm in the "global economy." And harm, as dehumanization of persons made in the image of God, needs to be apprehended through *other* than purely "rational" categories. Rubenstein explains how surplus production of goods and people, as identified by Hegel, is not a surprising anomaly or irregularity, symptomatic of systemic malfunction or dysfunction. It is intrinsic to what is a rational process, a side effect of it doing what it is supposed to do. This means that intervention on behalf of the poor, or for whatever "humane" pretext, must be construed as interference; it doesn't "make sense."

Such rationalizing dynamics are at work in a contemporary example concerning the World Bank's stated aim of the "greater integration of Africa into the world trading system," beginning with trade liberalization. In "Initiating Surrender," Dot Keet, researcher at the Centre for Southern Africa Studies, University of the Western Cape, cites a World Bank study document:

> "From a theoretical perspective that ignores social and political costs, the best solution is likely to be a rapid far-reaching unilateral liberalisation with commensurate exchange rate action. . . . Such an approach would supersede any need to specifically encourage regional economic integration." However, with widespread popular opposition to the imposition of IMF SAPS in Africa (and cogent criticisms by African organisations and international agencies of their socially and economically damaging effects), it is not easy for the World Bank to ignore totally the "social and political costs" its analysts refer to, or the "wide-ranging and politically difficult implications" of its generalised liberalisation proposals. Thus, the

study adopts what it calls "the pragmatic view" that liberalisation on a regional basis is a useful intermediate strategy because it "can yield more lasting and worthwhile results where unilateral liberalisation is being resisted."[35]

Rubenstein shows how intervention is seen to produce only "evil" effects that must be avoided in favor of rational solutions which do not interrogate or challenge the neutral (God-given?) premises of human rationalizing consciousness. He cites Hegel on the subject of public assistance, the necessity of foreign markets and territorial acquisitions. He explains the phenomenon of the construction of unreal people in a money economy:

As an alternative, they [the poor] might be given subsistence directly through being given work, i.e. the opportunity to work. In this event the volume of production would be increased, but the *evil* consists precisely in an excess of production and the lack of a proportionate number of consumers who are themselves also producers, and thus it is simply intensified by both the methods . . . by which it is sought to alleviate it. It hence becomes apparent that despite an excess of wealth civil society is not rich enough, i.e. its own resources are insufficient to check excessive poverty and the creation of a penurious rabble. . . .

The inner dialectic of civil society thus drives it . . . to push beyond its limits and seek markets, and so its necessary means of subsistence in foreign lands which are either deficient in the goods it has overproduced, or else generally backward in industry. . . . Civil society is thus driven to found colonies. Increase in population alone has this effect, but it is due in particular to the appearance of a number of people who cannot secure the satisfaction of their own needs by their own labour once production rises above the requirements of consumers. . . .

The object is here something that has meaning according to its [money] value, not for itself, not in relation to the need. . . . A person is real to the extent that he [or she] has money. . . . The formal principle of reason is to be found here . . . it is the

35. Dot Keet, "Initiating Surrender," *African Agenda* 1:4 (1995): 16.

abstraction from all particularity, character, historicity, etc. of the individual.[36]

An initial theological impasse accompanies a realization that indeed, for achieving the good of efficiency and competitiveness (e.g., in the Colombian context of small coal mines, where lack of capital and industrial infrastructure is the given reality), child labor *is* rational. Empirically, young boys *are* an ideal source of labor. Good, credible reasons for *not* using them must be grounded in different, competing philosophical or theological rationale. Such reasons need also to propose concrete economic alternatives that are locally and communally sustainable. This means that abstract affirmations of the "good creation" will need to be translated into concrete agendas that preserve creation as good, and nurture persons as real. They will need to find adequate expression for living faith, in living symbols. To do so in the context of the "global economy" means challenging and resisting the commonsense hegemony of economic, political, and cultural triage.

Two dissonance-heightening realities named by Rubenstein are relevant for this challenge. The first concerns an executive of a German corporation of the Nazi era, who was in charge of synthetic rubber and petrochemical operations, including I. G. Farben's operation at Auschwitz:

> My point in stressing Dr. Ter Meer's American corporate connections is not to suggest that corporate executives are possessed of some distinctive quality of villainy. It is to emphasize the extent to which the same attitude of impersonal rationality is required to run successfully a large corporation, a death camp slave labor factory and an extermination center.[37]

The second emerges in reflection on the "simple" point of triage:

> Within the logic of triage, there is nothing sacred about human life. It is simply another component to be calculated in amoral

---

36. Rubenstein, *Age of Triage*, 5-6.
37. Rubenstein, *Cunning of History*, 60.

cost-benefit analysis. Unfortunately, such thinking contains no credible constraint on its own excesses.[38]

This logic means that theological opposition to the dehumanization experienced and perceived in the "global economy" must engage "tough solutions" that can legitimate themselves — rationally, politically, and even theologically. Those who pursue them feel justified. Rubenstein illumines this self-understanding:

> Few situations can reinforce an elite's sense of class pride as one in which its members have the power secretly to play god and decide the fate of millions of ordinary men and women, while regarding themselves as exempt from the consequences of the awesome judgments they mete out.[39]

Rubenstein articulates and negates forcefully what he both apprehends and comprehends as harm. His analysis of the dynamics of human captivity within the fact and spirit of triage does not conclude that resistance to such harm, or anticipation of liberation from such harm is futile. Rubenstein seeks agents for a project of affirmative action on behalf of the human species. However, he is not disposed in a proactive way to recruit professional churchpersons for this purpose. This is because he believes that the required transformation of consciousness is such that what must be overcome is itself grounded in and grew out of a religious revolution. What must be transcended is precisely the revolution of consciousness that *led* to modernization in the first place. Looking for "men and women of credible inspiration," he admits:

> It is doubtful that it will originate with contemporary, Western-trained clergymen, theologians, or religious scholars. The theological training received by most religious leaders in the West, whether Protestant or Jewish, and to a certain extent Roman Catholic, is an expression of the same spirit of rationality which gave birth to the modern world. It is, for example, impossible to receive a theological degree from any mainstream Western insti-

38. Rubenstein, *Age of Triage*, 212.
39. Ibid., 215.

tution without studying the basic texts of the biblical religions as if they were literary documents to be investigated in the same spirit of rational, critical inquiry as any other historical document. . . . [I]t is impossible for Western religious communities to overcome this secularization of consciousness which, when carried to extreme, can lead to mass murder. The way they train their professionals is itself an expression of the same secularization process.[40]

However, this is a place where pastoral theology can be self-critical and proactive. It can claim its mandate to recover, correct, and expand the intellectual tradition that informs its task of developing theory and practice for the ministry of care. "Is there a way out?" Rubenstein asks. In terms of his own limited study, context, and perspective, he acknowleges "the limits of analysis," i.e., limits of both Marxist and theistic transformation. He calls for nothing other than a process of critical conversion that incorporates being born anew as truly human. His articulation of this process, excerpted in what follows, is an explicit challenge for pastoral theology:

Our historical experience has taught us that neither secular capitalist individualism nor collectivist communism excludes the kind of human desolation described in this essay. There simply has to be a better way for human beings to dwell together on this planet. . . . The story we have told is one of the extraordinary achievements and the terrible costs of human rationality in modern times. The worst cost has obviously been the incredible waste of human potential and indeed of life itself from the English enclosures of Tudor times, the Great Famine in Ireland, the Armenian massacres, and the destruction of the European Jews to genocide in Kampuchea and the millions upon millions of men and women who are today condemned, through no fault of their own, to the damnation of permanent worklessness.

Unlike other nations, both in the past and in our own century, the United States cannot solve the problem of mass unemploy-

40. Ibid., 234.

ment and other forms of population redundancy by sending its unwanted people elsewhere. Neither unending growth nor unending movement offers a solution. In this new political and social environment, our worst pollution may be what we do to ourselves. That is why a religious transformation is crucial. But, if it is to come, it must be an inclusive vision appropriate to a global civilization in which Moses and Mohammed, Christ, Buddha, and Confucius all play a role. We can no longer rest content with a humanity divided into the working and the workless, the saved and the damned, the Occident and the Orient. Our fates are too deeply intertwined. The call for religious transformation is in reality a call to conversion, a call to change ourselves. Our preachers have rightly told us that we must be converted, and that we must be born again. Unfortunately, what has been understood as conversion has all too often been devoid of the inclusive social component our times demand. In truth, we must be born again as men and women blessed with the capacity to care for each other here and now.[41]

Revisiting the Past

The challenge in this call for a religious conversion and transformation has particularity for Christians, and especially for theology mediated in the pastoral context of the Christian church. It involves the critical challenge of re-evangelization through conscientization, as faith redevelopment through humanization. This requires a critical revisiting of past patterns of faith formation where distorted objectifications of faith responses have often been reinforced. In such deformation, some persons are doomed to a deficit of being because of the surplus of meaning that has been claimed, especially for whiteness and maleness, in terms of superior rational and moral capacities. Ontological equilibrium can only be restored to humankind through critical recognition of what our own and others' experience of the past has been. This means engaging in a

---

41. Ibid., 238-40.

NO ROOM FOR GRACE

process of critical dialogue and discernment. It calls for listening to voices involved in the construction of the past; to voices who now speak for those who were silenced, excluded, or misrepresented in that constructed past. In the light of the foregoing discussion of theological impasse, it calls for a critical hearing of the following challenge from Hegel and Rubenstein:

> Before we conclude, let us recall another observation by Hegel: "[History is] the slaughter bench at which the happiness of peoples, the wisdom of states, and the virtues of individuals have been sacrificed. . . ." For Hegel, as for the Calvinists and the Social Darwinists, value and fact are one and all we are left with is the slaughter bench of history. If there is to be more it will not come from the thinker, the theorist, or the theologian. It can only come from men and women of authentic religious inspiration.[42]

Despite an often limited personal and corporate capacity for self-critical consciousness, Christians do make public confessions of faith; that "we are not alone,"[43] that we exist with and before God, with and before each other. When that confession becomes a concrete confession, Christians in the North may be able to re-encounter the "men and women of authentic religious inspiration" who are critical Christian partners in the South. Among such partners are those who, like John Pobee and Englebert Mveng, identify anthropological blocks (especially for Christians) to any rebirth of human capacity for mutual care. The following citation from Mveng functions as a bridge, between identification of this need for a critically renewed anthropology and analysis of Christian complicity in the construction of anthropological poverty. That such analysis is still necessary is evident in the reality that almost fifteen years have passed since Mveng uttered this challenge, in anticipation of an engaged respose:

> Let us face the facts: on the level of transition to praxis, reflection often lacks a certain maturity. We thank our colleagues for shar-

---

42. Ibid., 239.
43. United Church of Canada, "The New Creed," 1980.

ing with us, over the years, their Marxist analysis, their socialist projections for the society of the future, and their contextual reading of the Bible. But we are not satisfied. First of all, the basic problem remains the foundations of Western anthropology, which imposes itself upon the world. The concept of the human being that the West seeks to export to us is based on domination, power, death struggle, and so on — the triumph of death over life. There has never been a way to avoid an impasse. It is not easy to see how this can be reconciled with the gospel.

We hear of the church of the poor, and we are directed to the Beatitudes. But poverty is defined first of all in function of one's conception of the human being — and here we are back with anthropology again. Of course there is capital, of course there is the class struggle, of course there is the exploitation of human being by human being. And so of course there is a theology of violence, just as there is a theology of the rationality of the state. But for us Africans, the world's institutionalized poverty has other roots as well, and it is perhaps these other roots that are more serious, more important, and more relevant to the present moment: slavery, colonialism, neocolonialism, racism, apartheid, and the universal derision that has always accompanied the "civilized" world's discourse upon and encounter with Africa — and still accompanies it today.

. . . There is a type of poverty that I call, "anthropological poverty." It consists in despoiling human beings not only of what they have, but of everything that constitutes their being and essence — their identity, history, ethnic roots, language, culture, faith, creativity, dignity, pride, ambitions, right to speak . . . we could go on indefinitely.

There is a more serious form of impoverishment. It weighs not only upon Africa, but upon a very great proportion of humanity. This is the impoverishment that, when confronted with the gospel, is seen to be its negation pure and simple. It ought to constitute a serious subject for the reflection of theologians, because "anthropological impoverishment" can take on "theological" forms as well: it drains, voids, persons of everything that can enable them to recognize Christ as a person. Others have spoken of pseudo-evangelization. There is no need to repeat here what they have said. . . .

The New Delhi debates enabled us to recognize one another in the truth. It was too rich an experience for us to be able to set forth all its lessons here. The EATWOT theologians dispersed, rejuvenated and confirmed, with a vast program before it — whose most exciting point will be the January 1983 encounter of Third World theologians with their counterparts from the West. Turn the page. A new dialogue is about to begin.[44]

In the next chapter, I present voices from the past. I am trying to discern where critical resources are to be found for productive dialogue. This involves identifying obstacles that stand in the way of the expectations conveyed in Mveng's anticipation of response.

---

44. Englebert Mveng, "Third World Theology — What Theology? What World?: Evaluation by an African Delegate," in *Irruption of the Third World: Challenge to Theology*, ed. Virginia Fabella and Sergio Torres (Maryknoll, New York: Orbis Books, 1983), 220-21. This is a publication of papers from the Fifth International Conference of the Ecumenical Association of Third World Theologians (EATWOT), August 17-29, 1981, New Delhi.

CHAPTER THREE

Voices from the Past

Resources for Critical Faith Development

Retracing Steps

> *Yes*
> *our today's dance*
> *toward a better tomorrow*
> *is dictated by yesterday*[1]

A dance toward the better tomorrow of a rehumanized global economic context requires an understanding of yesterday's imprint on its steps. That imprint has rhythmic traces and motifs that are distinctively Christian. Analysis, interpretation, synthesis, and integration of historical materials can promote critical consciousness of Christianity's influence in the construction of the "global economy." Three general objectives govern what is here only an introductory sample of such materials.

First, retracing steps begins with documenting historical evidence and analyses of connections between Christian mission, European colonialism, Western capitalism, white racism, and cur-

---

1. Baleka Kgositsile, "Umkhonto," in *Malibonqwe: ANC Women: Poetry is Also Their Weapon*, ed. Sono Molefe (African National Congress, ca. 1983), 16.

55

rent experience of captivity within structural consequences of those connections.

Secondly, liberation for self-critical resistance against obstacles to a "better tomorrow" requires uncovering false steps. This means revisiting uncritical and/or distorted depictions of the past. Overcoming the danger of nurturing false consciousness through collusion in such depictions, calls for recognition of their tone and content and critical awareness of how they function.

Thirdly, materials have been selected with an objective of identifying critical sources of truth, in voices that record experiences of oppression, exclusion, and marginalization that have been caused, or at the least unmitigated by, patterns of Christian nurture and witness.

Serving the larger task of exploring implications of the "global economy" for pastoral theology and Christian faith development, this chapter is limited to providing historical context for tracing *origins* of dehumanization.

In personally selecting voices, I wish to avoid indirectly laying blame, pronouncing guilt, or pleading innocence. My intention is that the actual persons speak for themselves. I include samples of historical narrative, critical analysis, and emancipatory, rhetorical speech. Voices of "civilization's" charter members and entitled citizens, its resident aliens and excluded pariahs are represented. I introduce and engage different voices in order to show how the historical tradition reflects *both* Christianity's complicity *and* its critique of complicity in dehumanizing economic enterprises.

Discernible in the material cited are the phenomena of knowing, and wishing not-to-know, about systemic oppression. Witnesses and sources are cited verbatim in order to demonstrate both *why* the Christian tradition needs to be interrogated, and *how* it contains within itself hermeneutical resources for self-critical reflection. Voices of commentators, critics, victims, and perpetrators of harm are presented on the assumption that they are resources to be explored further in terms of their relevance for illuminating current realities. Conclusions drawn from this selective sample are necessarily preliminary and may serve to structure further research. What *is* being claimed decisively in this book is the importance of discerning, from the critical dynamics of the present social/pastoral context, those questions that lead to a critical appropriation of historical resources.

For Christians, discovering or rediscovering who and where we were is part of doing justice in the present, doing justice to the past (especially to the victims of the past), and envisioning new possibilities for a just future. Looking back can serve the task of developing theory and practice for the ministry of care, in economic realities in which the humanness of human life needs to be re-constituted and stabilized. In particular, it can provide historical perspective for mutually empowering pastoral relationships, where persons can recover, correct, and expand critical theological under-standings and faith commitments related to being human. This approach assumes that for caregivers and care-receivers in a pastoral context, this is a critical process. It involves recognizing, naming, and owning one's own personal/political identity (race, class, gender, etc.), in a historical continuum of dehumanizing power relationships.

Selecting Voices

Why one experience rather than another? Why this voice and not that one? Why this conclusion and not its counterpoint? I claim no vantage point *above* the "slaughter-bench of history" where, in my own voice or that of others, I can determine "fact and value as one" and presume to indict, convict, exonerate, or acquit persons and groups. However, in this chapter and throughout the book, I give hermeneutical and epistemological privilege to speech where I discern meanings that matter for critical faith redevelopment. For me such meanings are almost always concrete and contextual. They are characterized by an *apprehension* and *comprehension* of harm that both informs and empowers resistance and hope. Critical faith content is discernible to me in the voices of those who denounce harm to the fact and spirit of people's lives, and who announce that things can and must be different. I hear such voices in "women poets of South Africa," described by Sono Molefe:

[They] want your heart, eyes and nerves to move your mind to what they know, so that understanding afresh, you might be inclined to act accordingly. "We are exploited and oppressed," is what the collective voice states on behalf of those whose cries and words are muffled by bullet sounds plus fascist manoeuvres to bluff the unwitting. "We shall be free" is the tough fibre that binds those on both sides of the Apartheid divide.[2]

In selecting voices, I find guidance from three different quarters. The first, Sydney Ahlstrom, represents the voice of established historical scholarship. In what follows, he articulates the critical scope and responsibility of the conscientious historian:

> Each generation can only say that a different portion of the past is open for its examination, that its angle of vision is altered, and that new standards of explanation and relevance prevail. A new present requires a new past and the historian's responsibility for creating a meaningful past depends more on his [or her] interpretation of accepted historical knowledge than on his addition to the world's overflowing treasury of fact.[3]

The second, Elsa Tamez, represents the female voice of Mestiza experience of exclusion. Her voice contributes to creating the "new past" that the "new present" makes necessary. She provides hermeneutical criteria for the theological reconstruction of a meaningful past, on the basis of a "new logic of the Spirit." This way of *knowing better* provides a source of redemptive knowing. Old abstractions and new concrete meanings concerning life and death "in the Spirit" are dialectically engaged. The redeeming content of life beyond polarized existence, as victims and perpetrators or winners and losers, is projected in the following passage to which I return in later chapters. Here I am identifying rehumanized, eschatological hope, in a voice speaking from the historical experience of dehumanizing forces. In the case of Tamez, it is the experience

---

2. Molefe, *Malibonqwe*, 4.

3. Sydney E. Ahlstrom, *A Religious History of the American People* (New Haven and London: Yale University Press, 1972), 3.

of Spanish/Portuguese destruction of Mexico's indigenous populations:

> We concluded that, by declaring human beings to be just and making them just, justification by faith (understood as the historical action of God that makes concrete the revelation of God's justice) is good news for the thousands of excluded people of history. There are several reasons behind that conclusion.
>
> - By considering the solidarity of God as the root of justification, the excluded person is aware that God is present in solidarity in Jesus Christ, the excluded person par excellence, and also in all others who are excluded. This fact allows the excluded person to be aware that he or she bears the image of God. . . . Sisters and brothers celebrate in community together the gift of life that is granted by grace. Exclusion is condemned because all have received the right to a life of dignity.
> - Insofar as it is by faith and not by law that one is justified, the excluded person becomes aware of being a historical subject and not an object, either of the law or of a system that subjects her or him to marginalization. By being justified by faith in the one who raises the dead and brings to life that which does not exist, the excluded person is incorporated with new power into a new logic. . . . Faith in the resurrection of the body as the fulfillment of life on earth gives power to struggle and defend the life of all people.
> - Incorporated into the new logic of the Spirit, whoever has this faith forgets neither his or her past as a victim excluded by sin, nor the possibility that he or she too subjects others to exclusion. Such persons know that they have been accepted by God purely by the merciful solidarity of God, not because they are just. The death of the crucified one reminds them always of the cruelty of sin that kills with the full sanction of the law. When the solidarity of the Triune God — as friend and as brother or sister — is received by faith, this presence of God through

the Spirit turns into a permanent critical appeal to conscience in the paths of justice.[4]

Some Assigned Questions

My third source of guidance in selecting voices is Justo Gonzalez, who represents the voice of *critical* solidarity with "the current emphasis on 'globalization' in North American theological education":[5]

> I tend to share in what S. Mark Heim's paper calls, "a suspicion that globalization is an ideal formulated by Westerners in such a way that they alone have the means to be expert at it." In other words, that there is a form of "globalization" that, even if its proponents do not realize it, is one more way in which the West imposes its standards on the rest of the world, and then faults them for not meeting such standards.

This Cuban-born Protestant church historian names the structured "asymmetry" of a global Christian church that has yet to actualize an ecumenical sharing of resources. Gonzalez provides suggestions for globalizing theological education. His rationale challenges pastoral theology to be about mediating meaning, in pastoral relationship with *all* of God's creation:

> No amount of curriculum reform in the United States will suffice to change such "asymmetry," which is not the result of theological curriculum, but of international and national injustice — albeit an injustice that is often aided and abetted by the theological curriculum. Actually, to imagine that such asymmetry can be impacted significantly by curricular reform implies a gross underestimation of the asymmetry itself and its historical, structural and economic causes. . . . The purpose of globalization should

4. Elsa Tamez, *The Amnesty of Grace: Justification by Faith from a Latin American Perspective* (Nashville: Abingdon Press, 1993), 166.
5. Justo L. Gonzalez, "Globalization in the Teaching of Church History," *Theological Education* 29 (Spring 1993): 49.

be to produce graduates who can bring a global perspective to the particular situation in which they are serving. In the case of parish ministers . . . this implies helping the local church be aware that it is part of the church catholic — doing this through worship, preaching and teaching, bringing this to bear on ethical and political decisions, making it visible through the sharing of human and material resources etc. It also implies making the rest of the church present before the local congregation in such a way that its voice can be heard both in comfort and in challenge.[6]

Gonzalez's critical questions provide a hermeneutical framework for listening to other voices. They provide a critical model of theological affirmative action, a catechesis for the faith redevelopment of those of us who need to be empowered to hear.

How did it come about that the vast majority of Christians in today's world are poor?

How did it come about that most of us are not among them? On each side of the asymmetry how does that affect our understanding of Christianity, our life as a church, our relation with society, our relations with each other? . . . What economic, cultural, theological and other forces have created the sort of relationships in which we are all engaged?

Why are there churches in our part of the world that can engage in the sort of theological education that our seminaries provide, and others that cannot?

In the seemingly advantageous situation, what do we gain? What do we lose?

Until our courses are so structured that the asymmetry provides genuine opportunities for learning in both directions, the task of globalization in theological education will still remain to be done.[7]

6. Ibid., 50-51.
7. Ibid., 68.

Christian Entanglement in Imperial Culture

The Political Is Evangelical

Tracing Christian complicity in the construction of the economics and ideologies of global capitalism involves examining the phenomenon of Christian imperial culture. Instructive for this inquiry is the following premise of South African missiologist, Willem Saayman:

> The way in which the Christian community understands the political dimension of its mission also determines its understanding of the evangelical dimension.[8]

Bibliographical exploration of what Saayman analyzes as "the entanglement of mission and colonialism," reveals a complex of interlocking topics that need to be revisited and critiqued in the light of reflection on the "global economy." Such topics include:

- the Constantinian dispensation in the church/state relationship
- secular imperialism
- mutual influence of secular and religious expansion
- precedents in crusading wars against Islam
- Christianizing agendas of religious orders and monarchs
- official patronage of exploration and exploitation
- growth of European confidence, i.e., Renaissance, religious Reformation movements
- development of the sense of cultural/moral/religious superiority
- phenomena of entitlement and manifest destiny
- excesses, fanatical mission, gold fever
- psychological structures of innocence, good conscience

I do not develop these topics here. Rather, I am identifying what I

8. Willem Saayman, *Christian Mission in South Africa* (Pretoria: University of South Africa, 1991), 2.

62

assume to be relevant contextual background from which the characteristics and features of "entanglement" can be discerned.

How Did We Get Where We Are Now?

In posing this question, I speak in the collective voice of Christian and non-Christian critics, who share a sense that where Christians are now is problematic for Christians. Out of different social locations and degrees of physical/material security or privation, this collective voice raises faith issues. It asks who Christians are and what "we" can or cannot do to live credibly and authentically out of that identity, in our own life context. The particularity of the following contemporary Nicaraguan voice expresses such critical consciousness. It evokes the ethos of distorted socioeconomic relations and systemic captivity:

Voice: Miguel d'Escoto, Chair, Nicaraguan Foundation for Integral Community Development (FUNDECI), served as foreign minister to the Sandinista government and was suspended from the exercise of his priesthood.

> The economic situation in Nicaragua — in general, but particularly from the point of view of hunger — is even worse today than in the worst days of the Somoza years prior to the revolution. . . . I would say that the world is really sick with terminal selfishness. . . . We have to give testimony of Our Lord's love and concern for all human beings especially those who suffer the most. I ceased long ago to think of the organized church as an institution committed to those ideals. . . . We are crucifying him all over again, by silencing him inside of us. It's not anyone from outside doing this. It is we who silence him, because of fear. Fear of reprisals, or fear of whatever. Of those in authority, who may not be pleased. So we must pray to be free from the shackles of such fear.[9]

9. Miguel d'Escoto, *Catholic New Times* (February 19, 1995).

From the immediate past, the next voice also testifies to the scope of captivity that can be effected by ideological and political forces. From Africa, this collective voice speaks within historical earshot of d'Escoto. It reflects self-consciously on the events of a more distant past. It is the voice of those with recent memories of unarmed black children resisting security forces during the July '85–March '86 state of emergency in South Africa.

Voice: The "Concerned Evangelicals"

> Moreover, the situation was no more conducive to mass evange-listic campaigns and revivals [or public rallies, protests]. We could not execute our mission or fulfill our calling to the ministry [as] we were expected to do. . . .
> . . . Our frustration was that our own churches, groups or organizations were almost lost and could not provide prophetic light in the situation. At the worst most would be supporting the status quo instead of being a conscience to the state. We felt that although our perception of the gospel helped us to be what we are, saved by the blood of the Lord Jesus Christ, born again into the new family of the Kingdom of God, our theology nevertheless was inadequate to address the crisis we were facing. . . . We realized that our theology was influenced by American and European missionaries with political, social and class interests which were contrary to or even hostile to both the spiritual and social needs of our people in this country.[10]

Critically repentant, and conveying a sense of newly lost innocence, this confessional voice articulates the entangling connection between theology and concrete political reality.

Another voice provides a rationale for a historical analysis of the "political, social and class interests" that the "Concerned Evangelicals" have identified as the hostile *source* of their inadequate theology. More than a decade before, a voice had spoken out in the

10. "Concerned Evangelicals," *Evangelical Witness in South Africa: A Critique of Evangelical Theology and Practice by South African Evangelicals* (Grand Rapids, Michigan: Wm. B. Eerdmans Publishing Company), 17.

context of a critical mass of black African exploitation and oppression. From an earlier vantage point, this voice illumines what the "Concerned Evangelicals" had missed because of their limited way of knowing about who and whose they are as African Christians. This voice analyzes experience, makes a conclusive diagnosis, and prescribes radical treatment. The analysis anticipates the course of what has been experienced in Africa as a capitalist disease. Expressing a collective consciousness and a shared experience of suffering, the following voice communicates what is known by victims and survivors of economic/racial oppression and anthropological poverty. It reflects an analysis which is critically conscious of European colonialism. Christian complicity in race and class oppression can be seen here, not as a peculiar evil but as the accepted order of the day.

Voice: Walter Rodney, Third World historian, born in Guyana, 1942, and assassinated there in 1980

> This book derives from a concern with the contemporary African situation. It delves into the past only because otherwise it would be impossible to understand how the present came into being and what the trends are for the near future. In the search for an understanding of what is now called "underdevelopment" in Africa, the limits of inquiry have had to be fixed as far apart as the fifteenth century, on the one hand, and the end of the colonial period, on the other hand.
>
> Ideally, an analysis of underdevelopment should come even closer to the present than the end of the colonial period in the 1960s. The phenomenon of neo-colonialism cries out for extensive investigation in order to formulate the strategy and tactics of African emancipation and development. This study does not go that far, but at least certain solutions are implicit in a correct historical evaluation just as given medical remedies are indicated or contra-indicated by a correct diagnosis of a patient's condition and an accurate case history. Hopefully, the facts and interpretations that follow will make a small contribution towards reinforcing the conclusion that African development is possible only

on the basis of a radical break with the international capitalist system, which has been the principal agency of underdevelopment of Africa over the last five centuries.

*   *   *

Since capitalism, like any other mode of production, is a total system which involves an ideological aspect, it is also necessary to focus on the effects of the ties with Africa on the development of ideas within the superstructure of European capitalist society. In that sphere, the most striking feature is undoubtedly the rise of racism as a widespread and deeply rooted element in European thought. The role of slavery in promoting racist prejudice and ideology has been carefully studied in certain situations, especially in the U.S.A. The simple fact is that no people can enslave another without coming out with a notion of superiority, and when the colour and other physical traits of those people were quite different it was inevitable that the prejudice should take a racist form. . . . It can be affirmed without reservations that the white racism which came to pervade the world was an integral part of the capitalist mode of production. Nor was it merely a question of how the individual white person treated a black person. The racism of Europe was a set of generalisations and assumptions, which had no scientific basis, but were rationalised in every sphere from theology to biology.

Occasionally, it is mistakenly held that Europeans enslaved Africans for racist reasons. European planters and miners enslaved Africans for economic reasons, so that their labour could be exploited. Indeed, it would have been impossible to open up the New World and to use it as a constant generator of wealth, had it not been for African labour. There were no alternatives: the American (Indian) population was virtually wiped out and Europe's population was too small for settlement overseas at that time. Then, having become utterly dependent on African labour, Europeans at home and abroad found it necessary to rationalise that exploitation in racist terms as well. Oppression follows logically from exploitation, so as to guarantee the latter. Oppression of African people on purely racial grounds accompanied, strengthened and became indistinguishable from oppression for economic reasons. . . . There was always a contradiction between the elaboration of democratic ideas inside Europe and the elaboration of authoritarian and thuggish practices by Europeans with respect to Africans. . . . it is not even true to say that capitalism developed democracy at home in Europe and not abroad. At home, it was responsible for a talk or certain rhetoric of freedom, but it was never extended from the bourgeoisie to the oppressed workers; and the treatment of Africans must surely have made such hypocrisy a habit of European life, especially within the ruling class. How else can one explain the fact that the Christian church participated fully in the maintenance of slavery and still talked about saving souls?[11]

Christian self-understanding is discernible in those who have responded explicitly to the call to give an account of the faith that is in them. They include commentators, critics, victims, or perpetrators of oppression. They explain, interpret, defend, or indict the Christian tradition; they announce its truths and denounce its errors. From such dialectical material, recorded as "Christian History," "Church History," or "Western" political, economic, cultural, or social history, critical voices can be selected. They uncover roots of both dynamic and demonic connections between penultimate sacred agendas and historical secular contingencies. The roots are deep, nourished by Jewish and Christian experience of a relationship between God and humankind. Such historical discourse concerning human responsibility and accountability often invokes the testimony of scriptures. Communally interpreted, they have provided criteria for discerning, testing, and actualizing right relations between God and creatures made in the image of God. The following voice articulates a traditional understanding of and approach to this critical process.

Voice: *Jerome Biblical Commentary*

The limitations of Israelite morality have often been pointed out; they include the acceptance of slavery, polygamy, and divorce, the

11. Walter Rodney, *How Europe Underdeveloped Africa* (Harare, Zimbabwe: Zimbabwe Publishing House, 1972), vii, 7, 99-101.

double standard of sexual morality (stricter on women), a remarkably intense hatred of foreigners, inhumanity in war, and a certain laxness in regard to mendacity and theft. In these instances Israelite morality fails to rise entirely above the morality of its world, though even in these areas it is somewhat superior. A more refined moral insight should not be demanded as if morality were something that could be produced instantly; Israelite morality was not the creation of a few intellectuals but the code of behavior of an entire people, a folk morality in its development as in its origins. The remarkable feature of Israelite morality is that it contained the principles by which its limitations could be overcome.[12]

The voices which follow record critical accounts of what in the dominant historical tradition is usually characterized as "mission," "expansion," "exploration," or "development." I select voices that intentionally depict, not just *what* took place, but *how* events are interconnected in terms of cause and effect. These voices provide critical insight into how responsibility and accountability are located, for past human follies analysed then and now as colonialism, racism, and imperialism. Critical historical consciousness can interpret current experience of dehumanization and ideological captivity. It becomes understandable as a continuum of structured political and economic oppression, resistable now as in the past. This way of knowing produces a concious need to recover and appropriate the critical theological resources that empower concrete resistance. Those Jewish/Christian "principles," by which the "limitations" of the best intentions or uncritical conscience of the past can be overcome, may provide saving content for critical faith.

Voice: John Webster Grant, Canadian church historian

The missionary impulse is as old as Christianity itself, and indeed was prefigured by the Jewish quest for proselytes. It derived

12. *Jerome Biblical Commentary* (Englewood Cliffs, New Jersey: Prentice-Hall Inc., 1968), vol. 2, 757.

naturally from belief in one God who cares for all and has a claim on the allegiance of all. It took on new urgency when the conviction spread that the coming of Jesus, culminating in his death and resurrection, opened up new possibilities of fulfillment. This compulsion to spread the faith was strengthened still further by belief in a culmination of history yet to come. Only in the eschaton would the meaning of the cosmos be fully revealed and from early times it was widely believed that the millenial reign of Christ would come only when the Gospel had been diffused throughout the world. Christianity thus offered salvation to everyone regardless of accidents of birth and culture, while by the same token it claimed acceptance from everyone. . . .

The voyages of Columbus to America in 1492 and of Vasco da Gama to India in 1498 opened the world to European initiative, and within a few decades, thousands of preaching friars were seeking converts abroad. Secular and religious expansion were connected by intimate but complex ties of mutual influence. Secular imperialism was inspired by a European — or at any rate Latin — sense of mission that had a distinctly religious component: Columbus set off with the active backing of the primate of Spain and many other prominent members of the clergy. In turn, growing awareness of the outside world helped to stimulate a sense of mission on the part of the church. One of St. Ignatius's best-known exercises was simply a stretching of the imagination to encompass the activities and needs of different races in every part of the earth.[13]

Voice: Eduardo Galeano, Latin American writer-journalist

When Christopher Columbus headed across the great emptiness west of Christendom, he had accepted the challenge of legend. . . . Columbus took along a copy of Marco Polo's book and covered its margins with notes. . . . Out of Marco Polo's sparkling pages leaped all the good things of creation. There were nearly thirteen thousand islands in the Indian seas, with mountains of gold and

13. John Webster Grant, *Moon of Wintertime: Missionaries and the Indians in Encounter Since 1534* (Toronto: University of Toronto Press, 1984), 9, 10.

pearls and twelve kinds of spices in enormous quantities, in addition to an abundance of white and black pepper. . . . For Spain it was an era of reconquest: 1492 was not only the year of the discovery of America . . . but also of the recovery of Granada . . . the last Arab redoubt on Spanish soil. . . . But this was a holy war, a Christian war against Islam; and it was no accident that, in the same year of 1492, 150,000 Jews were expelled from the country. Spain achieved unity and reality as a nation wielding swords with the Sign of the Cross on their hilts. Queen Isabella became the patroness of the Holy Inquisition. The feat of discovering America can only be understood in the context of the tradition of crusading wars that prevailed in medieval Castile: the Church needed no prompting to provide a halo for the conquest of unknown lands across the ocean. Pope Alexander VI, who was Spanish, ordained Queen Isabella as proprietor and master of the New World. The expansion of the kingdom of Castile extended God's reign over the earth. . . . Three years after the discovery, Columbus personally directed the military campaign against the natives of Haiti, which he called Espanola. A handful of cavalry, two hundred foot soldiers, and a few specially trained dogs decimated the Indians. More than five hundred shipped to Spain, were sold as slaves in Seville and died miserably. Some theologians protested and the enslavement of Indians was formally banned at the beginning of the sixteenth century. Actually it was not banned but blessed: before each military action the captains of the conquest were required to read to the Indians, without an interpreter but before a notary public, a long and rhetorical *Requerimiento* exhorting them to adopt the holy Catholic faith:

> If you do not, or if you maliciously delay in so doing, I certify that with God's help I will advance powerfully against you and make war on you wherever and however I am able, and will subject you to the yoke and obedience of the Church and of their majesties and take your women and children to be slaves, and as such I will sell and dispose of them as their majesties may order, and I will take your possessions and do you all the harm and damage that I can. . . .

America was the vast kingdom of the Devil, its redemption impossible or doubtful; but the fanciful mission against the natives' heresy was mixed with the fever that New World treasures stirred in the conquering hosts. Bernal Diaz del Castillo, faithful comrade of Hernán Cortés in the conquest of Mexico, wrote that they had arrived in America "to serve God and His Majesty and also to get riches."[14]

Voice: Sydney E. Ahlstrom

American history begins on Thursday, 11 October 1492, and the circumstances are set down tersely in the journal of Christopher Columbus, "Admiral of the Ocean Sea, Viceroy and Governor of whatever territory he might discover."

> The course was W.S.W. and there was more sea than there had been during the whole of the voyage. . . . At two hours after midnight the land was sighted at a distance of two leagues. . . .

On the following day Columbus landed, took possession of this island in the name of King Ferdinand and Queen Isabella, and named it San Salvador (Holy Savior). To the assembled natives he gave "little red caps, and glass beads to put round their necks, and many other things of little value, which gave them great pleasure, and made them so much our friends that it was a marvel to see." He surmised that they would be "more easily freed and converted to our holy faith by love than by force." With an optimism that the Anglo-American experience of succeeding centuries would hardly justify, he also declared, "I believe that they would easily be made Christians, as it appeared to me that they had no religion." . . . After returning to Spain, Columbus made a final entry in his journal (15 March 1493) voicing that same confidence:

> I know respecting this voyage that God has miraculously shown his will, as may be seen from this journal, setting forth the numerous miracles that have been displayed in the voyage, and in me who was so long at the court of your Highnesses, working

14. Eduardo Galeano, *Open Veins of Latin America: Five Centuries of Pillage of a Continent* (New York and London: Monthly Review Press, 1973), 21-23.

in opposition to and against the opinions of so many chief persons of your household, who were all against me, looking upon this enterprise as folly. But I hope, in our Lord, that it will be a great benefit to Christianity, for so it has ever appeared.

Thus, in the very year that Granada's fall terminated "the Last Crusade," the vista for another vast campaign opened before the rulers of Spain.[15]

For contemporary Canadians, who have diverse racial and ethnic histories, tracing how "we" got where "we" are means encountering each other in the context of a continuum of historical power imbalances. What follows is the collective voice of a "we" whose particular story of origin shows that critical issues will arise in such encounters.

Voice: Wayn Hamilton, Nova Scotian of African descent, has split his working time between West Africa and Canada.

While searching for the right glue to keep us — people of African descent — together, we must remind ourselves that we had a beginning as a people not in Nova Scotia, not in Canada, not in North America, but in Africa. Others have sacrificed a great deal for us to be here today. We must remember we have a connection to a specific past. Our connections go back many generations, many thousands of years. We are here because our ancestors survived. They survived and so must we. If people, no matter what colour, were inspired by Black History Month and had a chance to see our culture, our heritage, our contributions, it will help.

Someone once asked me what it is like to live in Africa. That's a difficult question to answer. Suppose you were to visit your great-grandmother — someone you had never seen before, but heard stories about. You would try, in a short while, to really get to know her. You would try to understand her, knowing that the things she did were rooted in ways handed down in centuries

15. Ahlstrom, *Religious History of the American People*, 36-37.

past — passed on to her from her mother, and her mother's mother. You would try to understand how she saw the world, share her hopes and dreams, and know she still had a lot to offer. You would sense there were problems with how others understood her situation. You would also come to understand her vision of the future, one filled with hope and promise.

You would watch her do the daily tasks, watch her give advice. You would participate in various activities she thought were important for you to experience, and listen as she spoke to her children. You would be amazed at how she maintained her courage, determination, hope and pride among so much hardship. For me, living in Africa is, in a lot of ways, like visiting my great-grandmother. As a Canadian of African descent, I am trying to embrace and reclaim elements of the heritage, history and culture in the widest possible way — getting to know the diaspora, the ethos of Africanism, attempting to understand the situation of a people whose past has been lost, stolen, or has strayed. . . .

We have to realize we have things in common with other people in the world. We have the same adversaries. We have the same problems to overcome. A poor person in Nova Scotia faces the same obstacles and barriers as the poor Sierra Leonean. Ask: Why is the Nova Scotian poor, or unable to improve quality of life, or why are the benefits of a full life only available for a small percentage of the population? Why are people living on the streets of Halifax and Freetown? Why is there a fishing crisis in Nova Scotia and one looming just around the corner here in Sierra Leone? If you look for a balanced answer, I'm sure you will be amazed at the similarities in the problems and potential solutions.[16]

In his image of visiting Africa as a great-grandmother, Wayn Hamilton provides an interpretive bridge. For another "we," i.e., Canadians of white Anglo-Saxon Protestant descent, does "trying to embrace and reclaim elements of [our] heritage, history, and

16. Wayn Hamilton, "Facing the Future, By Connecting with the Past," *Halifax Chronicle-Herald*, March 3, 1995.

culture *in the widest possible way"* mean that we need to be in critical dialogue with Hamilton's great-grandmother as well as our own?

Nurture in Innocence

At this point I need to address the identity of white Anglo-Saxon Protestant Canadians, in the dominant tradition of the "New World." It seems to me that family, church, and school have collaborated institutionally in the religious, political, and social formation of many Canadian Christians. I am proposing that for white Anglo-Saxon Protestants especially, this has been an experience of nurture in innocence, in habits of avoidance and denial. *Collective* identity has been shaped by tactful silence and discreet euphemism concerning historical connections between Christian mission, colonialism, capitalism, and racism. This means that for us, relinquishing a conditioned good conscience is an ideological/spiritual prerequisite for critical consciousness. It is a necessary first step toward liberation for self-critical resistance in a dehumanizing "global economy" that claims hearts and minds, body and spirit.

My own social location is that of a white, middle-class, Anglo-Saxon Protestant, born in 1941. My operating assumption is that Canadians like myself have been educated in the cultural middle-ground between the ethos of "British Empire" and "American manifest destiny." This produces a collective sense of being neither the heroes nor the villains of history. It has fostered and sustained a "good-guy" self-image, one of innocent good will. Like our ethnic counterparts in the U.S.A., Australia, New Zealand, and South Africa, we belong to those who arrived in the "New World" as entitled "settlers," with a subcontract from the "Motherland" to civilize, Christianize, and modernize those peoples who occupied territories already claimed for "us" by imperial forces. We are the descendants of an "ethnic" group that related to indigenous (and colonial/missionary rivals) as objects of outright elimination, economic exploitation, and/or conversion and assimilation. Our formal schooling has conditioned us to identify with the cultural assets, the industrial and technological prowess of "Great Britain." It has provided tacit approval for the accumulation of primary capital achieved by British imperial conquest. This has allowed us to distance ourselves, as minor actors, from any frontline atrocities. We have internalized "our" heritage of material benefits, as merited entitlements, without acknowledging the human costs as moral liabilities. We understand ourselves as neither perpetrators nor victims of war, genocide, slavery, apartheid, or holocaust. Such an ideological ethos can be discerned in the following passages from an historical account and explanation of the "Expulsion of the Acadians":

> Nova Scotia, called Acadia by the French, was the first part of the Dominion which came into permanent possession of Great Britain. It was ceded by Louis XIV to Queen Anne by the Treaty of Utrecht, in 1713. . . . For a long time after the cessation of Nova Scotia, the English found it difficult to maintain their authority in the Province. Its inhabitants, the Acadians, were of French origin, and Roman Catholics; they were unwilling to submit to British rule, and refused either to leave the country or to take the oath of allegiance, as required by the Treaty of Utrecht. Great forebearance was shown to them; but they would take no oath of allegiance except to their "good King of France"; and they were frequently found in league with the native Indians in armed resistance to British authority. . . . Instigated by their priests, they, along with the Indians, continued to annoy the new settlers [colonists from England and Protestants recruited from Europe]. Conspicuous among the fomenters of disaffection was the Abbé De La Loutre, who had been sent as a missionary to the Mic-Mac Indians. . . . As the Acadians could not be persuaded or compelled to become loyal British subjects, it was at last deemed necessary to expel them from the country. . . . The manner in which they were surprised, seized, forced into ships, and scattered among strangers [in the older English colonies in the south] has been severely criticized. On the other hand, their removal has been justified, as having been rendered necessary by their persistent disaffection and frequent acts of hostility. . . . Their deportation . . . was a political and military necessity. . . . To people the vacant lands which the exiled Acadians had cultivated, and

to strengthen the British power, settlers were invited to come to Nova Scotia from the older English colonies in North America.[17]

With the current momentum to level the playing field of global competition and achieve "harmonization," the logic of global market forces overrules any prior claims to cultural or racial privilege. Our cultural heritage of white Anglo-Saxon entitlement ill-prepares us historically, ethically, and psychologically to cope with being relativized, declassed, or de-skilled in a worldwide labor market. This produces alienation, which generates spontaneous anger and backlash (e.g., tax revolt, racism). Such psychic distress and the diminishment of historically privileged Canadians succeeds in distracting attention from, or subverting commitment to, historically marginalized groups. They now face being rendered surplus and effectively expendable. In this social and pastoral context, Christians in Canada are challenged to engage in self-critical analysis. Nurtured by uncritical versions of our past, we need to become aware of individual and collective false consciousness. We can learn to process our fears through conscious structural analysis and theological reflection. We can integrate fear positively, by apprehending *harm* in the dis-grace of backlash against the vulnerable (e.g., refugees, poor, unemployed, persons of color). We can seek comprehension of such harm through the grace of experiencing shared vulnerability and common cause against a common economic threat. This calls for resources from critical historical scholarship and from allies who are experienced in resisting dehumanization.

Recovery, Correction, and Expansion of Perspective

From Whom Can We Learn the Truth?

The critical recovery of an historical record of dissonant voices provides evidence that for some Christians, and many others,

17. William Gregg, *History of the Presbyterian Church in Canada* (Toronto: Presbyterian Printing and Publishing Company, 1885), 55-58.

economic exploitation and death have been by-products of forms of Christian practice and tradition. At a time of escalating global dehumanization, such voices provide resources for Christians to gain insight about the church's complicity in the global economy.

Voice: Rev. Dr. Ulrich Duchrow, regional secretary for mission and ecumenism, Evangelical Church of Baden, Heidelberg, Germany

> With the conquest of America from 1492 on, modern history begins as a world history defined by Europe. It is characterized by the capitalist system, which takes different shapes as different subjects follow the basic principle of utilizing capital to achieve profit. The main actors are banking, trading and industrial companies which, with changing political and social allies in Europe (and later in the US and Japan as well), build centres of power with the help of which the whole world is increasingly made capitalist. Knowledge of the capitalist world system and also of the resistance to it is indispensable for responsible action today. . . .
>
> It is equally important to be aware of the ideological legitimations with which this system was justified. For the most part they are still used today. The role of churches, missions and theologies has also been significant. . . . We can learn from the success and failure of forms of resistance in earlier centuries.
>
> > [Gustavo Gutiérrez:] Thus I say of these Indians, that these mines, treasures and riches were a means of their predestination and redemption; for we see clearly that, wherever they are, the gospel comes in plenty and with eagerness. Yet where there are none, just poor people, this is a means of rejection, for there the gospel never goes, since, as experience abundantly teaches, no soldier or general will go to a land without this endowment of gold and silver, and also no preacher of the gospel.
> >
> > [Bartolomé de Las Casas:] The sole and true root cause why the Christians murdered and destroyed such an enormous mass of guiltless people was simply this, that they sought to take into their power their gold. Their wish was to enrich themselves with treasures in a few days and thus to rise higher than their station and connections allowed.

[Gutiérrez:] It happened that a chieftain called all his people together. Each should bring whatever gold he had, and all of it should be placed together. And he said to his Indians: Come, friends, this is the god of the Christians. For we will dance before it for a while, then go to the sea and throw it in. When they find that we no longer have their god, they will leave us in peace.

[Las Casas:] The cazique (on a pyre in Cuba) . . . asked the priests whether Christians went to heaven too. Certainly, said the priests, all good Christians go there! Immmediately and without thinking the cazique replied that he would not wish to go there, but rather to hell, lest he should see more only the same cruel people, nor have to stay where they were. . . .

Robbery and murder of the peoples of America, Africa and Asia is the basis of Europe's wealth and world leadership. There is a mass of literature on the subject, and the angle from which the books are written is important. School text-books usually narrate these events from the Eurocentric viewpoint of the victors; it smoothes the rough edges. Thus we read of the "discovery of America," not the conquest and plundering of this continent. . . . But there are also books written from the viewpoint of the victims and of resistance.[18]

Las Casas, Gutiérrez, and Duchrow provide evidence that experience of oppression can and does find a voice and that subjugated voices are recoverable. This demonstrates that those nurtured in power and privilege are not congenitally incapable of hearing those voices. White Anglo-Saxon Protestant Canadians can therefore be assured that the deconstruction of unwarranted good conscience and the reconstruction of critical historical consciousness is possible and necessary. We need to appropriate historical resources in which we can discover the difference between what the tradition

18. Ulrich Duchrow, *Europe in the World System 1492-1992: Is Justice Possible?* (Geneva: WCC Publications, 1992), 3-4. Duchrow's English translator, Keith Archer, notes: "Duchrow . . . challenges me to look at the world not as how it appears from the British Isles but from the heart of the European continent. That sets British (and American) history in the wider context of Europe's dealings with the rest of the world over the last five hundred years."

told or tells us, and what actually happened. A critical version of who "we" were and are can be discerned in the voices of those who have been subjugated both *in* the past, and by versions *of* the past. Such experience finds a voice through scholars whose firsthand, contextual, or vicarious experience has caused them, in some degree, to internalize a preferential option for the oppressed. This critical hermeneutic begins to interrogate and inform their work.

I select the following voices to reflect a spectrum of critical historical perspectives that implicitly and explicitly give hermeneutical privilege to silenced majorities. The voices project different individual and collective identities. They reflect diverse experience of oppression and personal privilege. I wish to convey the epistemological dynamics of an ongoing critical process, where experience of oppression comes to expression, is recognized and *acknowledged as real*. Filling in gaps and silences — challenging, contradicting, or denouncing the master narratives of historical tradition — the subjugated views begin to participate in reconstructing the tradition.

Critical historical consciousness is very much a matter of having eyes to see and ears to hear. It is not simply new factual data which cause a historian to experience the need for creating a more meaningful past. Rather, it seems to come from experiencing the present in a critically new way. Feminists describe this phenomenon as seeing the same thing differently. This is also an experience of *needing* to know more and to know better, because of, or in spite of, what one has found out. The voices I present here demonstrate the possibility of overcoming fear of knowing and transcending a need not-to-know. I commend them as resources for the task of seeking and appropriating the truth about complicity in oppression and oppressive structures.

Voice: Eduardo Galeano

The division of labor among nations is that some specialize in winning and others in losing. Our part of the world, known today as Latin America, was precocious: it has specialized in losing ever since those remote times when Renaissance Europeans ventured across an ocean and buried their teeth into the throats of the Indian civilizations. Centuries passed, and Latin America has perfected its role. We are no longer in the era of marvels when fact surpassed fable and imagination was shamed by the trophies of conquest — the lodes of gold, the mountains of silver. But our region still works as a menial . . . and after all, as Alliance for Progress coordinator Covey T. Oliver said in July 1968, to speak of fair prices is a "medieval" concept, for we are in the era of free trade.

*   *   *

The ghosts of all the revolutions that have been strangled or betrayed through Latin America's tortured history emerge in the new experiments, as if the present had been forseen and begotten by the contradictions of the past. History is a prophet who looks back: because of what was, and against what was, it announces what will be. And so this book, which seeks to chronicle our despoliation and at the same time explain how the current mechanisms of plunder operate, will present in close proximity the caravelled conquistadores and the jet-propelled technocrats; Hernán Cortés and the marines; the agents of the Spanish Crown and the International Monetary Fund missions; the dividends from the slave trade and the profits of General Motors. And, too, the defeated heroes and revolutions of our time, the infamies and the resurrected hopes: the fertile sacrifices.

*   *   *

In the Middle Ages a small bag of pepper was worth more than a man's life, but gold and silver were the keys used by the Renaissance to open the doors of paradise in heaven and of capitalist mercantilism on earth. The epic of the Spaniards and Portuguese in America combined propagation of the Christian faith with usurpation amd plunder of native wealth. European power stretched out to embrace the world.

*   *   *

Ideological justifications were never in short supply. The bleeding of the New World became an act of charity, an argument for the faith. With the guilt, a whole system of rationalization for guilty consciences was devised.

80

*　　*　　*

In the seventeenth century Father Gregorio Garcia detected Semitic blood in the Indians because, like the Jews, "they are lazy, they do not believe in the miracles of Jesus Christ, and they are ungrateful to the Spaniards for all the good they have done them." At least this holy man did not deny that the Indians were descended from Adam and Eve: many theologians and thinkers had never been convinced by Pope Paul III's bull of 1537 declaring the Indians to be "true men." When Bartolomé de Las Casas upset the Spanish Court with his heated denunciations of the conquistadores' cruelty in 1557, a member of the Royal Council replied that Indians were too low in the human scale to be capable of receiving the faith. Las Casas dedicated his zealous life to defending the Indians against the excesses of the mine owners and *encomenderos*. He once remarked that the Indians preferred to go to hell to avoid meeting Christians.

*　　*　　*

The Indians have suffered, and continue to suffer, the curse of their own wealth; that is the drama of all Latin America.

*　　*　　*

During Holy Week, processions of the heirs of the Mayas produce frightful exhibitions of collective masochism. They drag heavy crosses and participate in the flagellation of Jesus step by step along the interminable ascent to Golgotha; with howls of pain they turn His death and His burial into the cult of their own death and their own burial, the annihilation of the beautiful life of long ago. Only there is no Resurrection at the end of their Holy Week.[19]

More recently, Galeano has provided further insight into his own self-understanding and vocation, as a writer eager to make the past known more and known better:

I am not a historian. I am a writer who would like to contribute to the rescue of the kidnapped memory of all America, but above

19. Galeano, *Open Veins of Latin America*, 11, 18, 24, 52, 53, 59, 62.

all of Latin America, that despised and beloved land: I would like to talk to her, share her secrets, ask her of what difficult clays she was born, from what acts of love and violation she comes.[20]

Voice: Sydney Ahlstrom

The land which England was now poised to occupy was vaster and richer than anyone then knew; but the English would discover only very slowly that its wealth was not like that which had dazzled Cortez and Pizarro. The material abundance, so decisive in shaping the character of future Americans, was not there for the taking; it would have to be produced by an industrious people — and their slaves. Between the dream and the achievement of a flourishing colonial empire, however, was the Indian.

The British knew, of course, that the terrain of the future United States was already inhabited. In fact, the conversion of heathen tribes would figure prominently among the stated objectives of imperial expansion in the New World, and long-lasting stereotypes of the Indians, as well as of the newly discovered Africans, were already taking shape. Yet nobody knew or could have guessed how diverse these indigenous people were, or how resistant to conversion and incorporation they would be. As for the Indians — who have so often been depicted standing on the shore in friendly expectation as a sailing ship hove into view — they even less could have imagined that ships would not stop coming until the greatest folk migration since the Germanic invasions of Europe had brought over forty-five million rapidly multiplying people to America. . . . "The hunting economy of the red man," writes one sympathetic and experienced scholar [Gustavus E. E. Lindquist, 1944], "was doomed from the moment that prancing Arab chargers were taken off the Spanish caravels; from the moment that the crude cannon and muskets of Champlain sounded out across the waters of the lake that bears his name. It was a doom slow in progress, but as inevitable as the procession of day and night."[21]

20. Eduardo Galeano, *Memory of Fire: Genesis* (New York: Pantheon Books, 1985), xv.
21. Ahlstrom, *Religious History of the American People*, 100.

Voice: John Webster Grant

Surveying the position of the churches among the Indians of Canada today, one could easily conclude that the story told in this volume belongs essentially to the past. . . . The outlook for Christianity does not seem promising. Yet an analysis of encounter in the past may warn us against closing the books prematurely. . . . It may yet prove, however, that the emergence of angry Indians capable of articulating their criticisms of the missions is precisely the catalyst needed to make possible the fruitful encounter between Christianity and Indian culture that has somehow always failed to take place. The factor most seriously inhibiting the transmission of Christianity in the past, I have argued, was a disparity in power between the senders and receivers of the message. In setting the terms on which Christianity would be accommodated into native societies the missionaries had to concede almost nothing, the Indians almost everything.[22]

Voice: Walter Rodney

The subject of Africa's contribution to European development reveals several of the factors which limit a writer's representation of reality. Language and nationality, for instance, are effective barriers to communication. Works in English seldom take into account of the effect brought about in France, Holland or Portugal by participation in slaving and other forms of commerce which exploited Africa in the pre-colonial period. The ideological gulf is responsible for the fact that most bourgeois scholars write about phenomena such as the Industrial Revolution in England without once mentioning the European slave trade as a factor in the primary accumulation of capital. . . .

Strictly speaking, the African only became a slave when he reached a society where he worked as a slave. Before that he was first a free man and then a captive. . . . On the whole, the process by which captives were obtained on African soil was not trade at all. It was through warfare, trickery, banditry and kidnapping.

22. Grant, *Moon of Wintertime*, 264-65.

When one tries to measure the effect of European slave trading on the African continent, it is very essential to realize that one is measuring the effect of social violence rather than trade in any normal sense of the word.

*　　*　　*

The penetration of foreign capitalism on a world-wide scale from the late nineteenth century onwards is what we call "imperialism." Imperialism meant capitalist expansion. It meant that European (and North American and Japanese) capitalists were forced by the internal logic of their competitive system to seek abroad in less developed countries opportunities to control raw material supplies, to find markets, and to find profitable fields of investment. The centuries of trade with Africa contributed greatly to that state of affairs where European capitalists were faced with the necessity to expand in a big way outside of their national economies. . . . Imperialism is essentially an economic phenomenon, and it does not necessarily lead to direct political control or colonialisation. However, Africa was the victim of colonialisation. In the period of the notorious "Scramble for Africa," Europeans made a grab for whatever they thought spelt profits in Africa. . . . The gap that had arisen during the period of pre-colonial trade gave Europe the power to impose political domination on Africa.[23]

Walter Rodney's findings concerning national/cultural and ideological impediments to "communication" reinforces a critical comment by John Pobee, that "communication is more effective when we pursue an error which is real to other people rather than a truth of which we are convinced.[24]

Voice: James Leatt et al.

The influence of Christianity in Africa is today a controversial issue. In some eyes missionaries were agents of imperialism, even

23. Rodney, *How Europe Underdeveloped Africa.*
24. Pobee, *Worship of the Free Market and the Death of the Poor,* 28.

racism. It was common in the nineteenth century for missionaries, administrators, and philanthropists in England — home of a vast empire of 500 million, spanning a large part of the globe — to view their culture as the pinnacle of man's achievements. Wilberforce, for example, when speaking of the colonies, ascribed their acquisition to "our religious and moral superiority." Robert Moffat after twenty years among the Tswana could not bring himself to believe they had any real religious apprehension. Such attitudes reflected a universal pride in Anglo-Saxon culture, which elevated the European to the top of the evolutionary ladder. Some would argue that this sense of superiority on the part of the English was not racial, although there is convincing evidence to the contrary. Such feelings of superiority were no doubt reinforced by the fact that when the English came to South Africa racial stereotypes already existed, and racial domination by whites was already established. The missionary was a child of the time and imbibed the superior and paternalistic attitudes of his culture. Western civilisation seemed so demonstrably superior in its technology, industry, literacy, political institutions, and weapons. In addition the missionary saw himself as a messenger of truth, and found it difficult to distinguish between cultural imperialism and the proclamation of the gospel.

The upper classes of Europe felt themselves called to govern and to spread "civilisation," and this is reflected in the attitudes of the European-based missionary societies and their policies abroad. The colonial church was paternalistic, showed deference to civil authority, and used its influence to advance the cause of the colonial government. . . . Even the sharpest critics of the colonial church would not wish to underrate the labours of the missionary in education, medicine, and evangelism. The record speaks for itself. But from a black perspective missionaries "consciously or unconsciously sought to Europeanise us before they would Christianise us. They have consequently jeopardised the entire Christian enterprise since . . . they have tended to make us feel somewhat uneasy and guilty about what we could not alter . . . *our Africanness*" (Bishop Tutu). Institutions such as Lovedale and Zonnebloem created syllabi with the express intention of making the scholar a replica of his English or Scottish counterpart. In effect, however, this educational policy appears to have had little detrimental long-term effect, save that syllabi still tend to be western in orientation — a legacy which even the theological seminaries have only recently begun to correct.[25]

Voice: Justo L. Gonzalez, Cuban church historian

A third "globalizing" influence was my own Latin American background and setting. Why is it, I asked myself, that the theology of Francisco de Vitorio, for instance, is usually ignored in histories of Christian thought? And even more, combining this with the ecumenical factor, why is it that most books on the history of theology or on church history — including most Roman Catholic books — give the impression that the only significant events of the sixteenth century were the Protestant and Catholic Reformations, some even totally ignoring the conquest of the Western Hemisphere, the debates surrounding it . . . ?[26]

Voice: Mercy Oduyoye, Deputy General Secretary, World Council of Churches

The challenges of having a global conversation are many, the economics put the Third World at a disadvantage. Europe and North America . . . can simply walk into Africa and begin to research and write on Africa. The reverse is not envisaged and has not been possible.[27]

Where Is Hope to Be Found?

In the "global economy," restructuring corporate enterprises, breaking social contracts, and privatizing public services may pro-

25. James Leatt et al., eds. *Contending Ideologies in South Africa* (Grand Rapids, Michigan: Wm. Eerdmans, 1986), 60-63.
26. Gonzalez, "Globalization in the Teaching of Church History," 64.
27. Mercy Oduyoye, "Contextualization as a Dynamic in Theological Education," *Theological Education* 30 (Autumn 1993): 120.

vide jobs. But there is no economic security. The common good is actively underdeveloped by a perverse but rational process in which privatization produces privation. The impact of this process on the real lives of real persons takes a corresponding toll on the actual faith of actual people.

The brutal reality of contingent work and chronic anxiety challenges the Christian church in terms of its historical relationship to power and its gospel understanding of human contingency and divine constancy. Thus far, this book has explored dimensions and patterns of Christian complicity in a dehumanizing phenomenon of global capitalism. Evidence has been presented to demonstrate that appropriations of the gospel have, in the past, proven to be dehumanizing. They have dealt death to those whose humanity was not recognizable, or was expendable, in the eyes of others caught up in the entanglement between mission and colonial exploitation, racism, and oppression. What about current rational projects and their threat to the human condition? What grounds are there for hoping that the *limitations* of contemporary visions of growth and progress, pursued with the best intentions and in good conscience, can be overcome with any greater success than those of the past? A caveat and some instructive criteria can be discerned in words from Simone Weil:

> We need first of all to have a clear conscience. Let us not think that because we are less brutal, less violent, less inhuman than our opponents we will carry the day. Brutality, violence, and inhumanity have an immense prestige that schoolbooks hide from children, that grown men do not admit, but that everyone bows before. For the opposite virtues to have as much prestige, they must be actively and constantly put into practice. Anyone who is merely incapable of being as brutal, as violent, and as inhuman as someone else, but who does not practice the opposite virtues, is inferior to that person in both inner strength and prestige, and he [or she] will not hold out against such a confrontation.[28]

28. Cited by Lewis H. Lapham, "Seen But Not Heard — The Message of the Oklahoma Bombing," *Harper's Magazine* (July 1995): 34. Lapham docu-

Weil's insights provide incentive to invest hope in the redemptive knowing of the victims and survivors of Christian complicity in past and current economic injustice. Is it not those who "hold out" and have held out, who may know more, or know better? Their critical resources can be recognized and appropriated for the faith development/redevelopment of others who need to learn how to resist capitulation to acceptable powerlessness. This can be undertaken in the spirit of claims made for the faith knowledge of those who have withstood confrontation with Christian and colonial forces. Such a spirit animates Eduardo Galeano, who claims that "the god of the pariah is not always the same as the god of the system that makes them pariahs."[29] It also confirms insights from historian David Barrett, who, back in 1968, wrote concerning the phenomenon of an emerging independent church movement in Africa:

> Outside the sphere of these orthodox Protestant and Catholic churches in Africa, something new of immense power and creativity is coming into being; and if, as I believe, it is a creation of the Spirit of God, proclaiming a new word of God from the Bible we thought we had fully understood, then we ignore it at our peril. . . . For a Christian theology, if it is to be truly Christian, must not rest merely on past formulations but must be a reflection on what God is doing in the present.[30]

Lewis Lapham claims that "what we hold in common is a unified field of emotions and a willingness to trust the reports of the other pilgrims on the road."[31] Is such trust not an ingredient of the critical faith that can ground a rereading of the pastoral context of the "global economy?"

---

ments the citation as "a fragment of an uncompleted manuscript that Simone Weil wrote down on a scrap of paper in 1939."

29. Galeano, *Open Veins of Latin America*, 99.

30. David Barrett, *Schism and Renewal in Africa* (Nairobi: Oxford University Press, 1968), xix.

31. Lapham, *Harper's Magazine* (July 1995): 35.

CHAPTER FOUR

Rereading the Context

Faith Development as Redevelopment

Why Is This Important?

Voices that speak in this book are selected from my own perspective of critical awareness of a phenomenon of Western Christian ideological captivity. The white Anglo-Saxon Protestant variation of innocence and good conscience, in which I was raised as a Canadian, receives specific attention. Personally and corporately, I experience "our" need for the appropriations of the Christian gospel of those who have resisted and continue to resist being dehumanized by consequences of "our" ideology. Such appropriations and critical reappropriations testify and witness to redemptive knowing. This kind of critical knowing is faith knowledge which both produces, and is a product of, *a new way of seeing*. It has an experiential basis for rereading life contexts which have been read, named, and endured as oppression, dis-grace, and unredemption. Thanks to critical scholars and mission partners, Christian faith knowledge acquired from subjugated existence is being recovered, reclaimed, and affirmed as revelatory and liberating. It can empower the pastoral project of reconstituting *all* persons as humans made in the image of God, in spite of how we or they may be "necessarily" defined in the logic of the "global economy." In my view, those who actualize such critical faith can be commended as channels of grace.

I believe that channels of grace are accessible through *conscious* experience of economic and ideological captivity that is acknowledged, shared, and analyzed. It can happen interpersonally and dialogically, between "winners" and "losers" in the "global economy." This experiential, contextualized, theological process is one which I explore in this chapter, in terms of faith development, underdevelopment, and redevelopment. It is a process of both recovering and discovering critical faith. As redemptive knowing, such faith is an indispensable, dynamic resource for reading the context of the "global economy." This is a function of both theological awareness and social literacy:

> Social illiteracy means being unable to read — to interpret the events that are going on in society. Unfortunately, many institutions do not teach Canadians to read social reality. A good percentage of the population remains unaware of how society works or where it is headed.[1]

A critical reading of the "global economy," as dehumanizing and as evil, is not an end in itself. It demoralizes and paralyzes unless it precipitates a rereading in which the local/global context is theologically reclaimed as part of a redeemed creation. Then, the discerned presence of evil, apprehended and comprehended as harm, can animate a faith response of resistance. One may ask: Who am I? For what and from what do I need to be saved? Who/what will save me? Such questions are personal, political, and hence theological/evangelical. Individually and corporately, Christians need to know well the reality of *both* Jesus' summons to personhood *and* the market's summons to squander personhood.

Critical consciousness forms and re-forms the will, the imagination and the productive hatred/love needed to inspire re-visioning. Without a vision of the dehumanized global context as re-

---

1. Michael Czerny and Jamie Swift, *Getting Started on Social Analysis in Canada*, second edition (Toronto: Between the Lines Publishing Company, 1988), 56.

humanized, anticipation of liberation can be displaced by capitulation to the spirit of inevitability. Rereading our own context as already globalized begins with reading ourselves and others through the eyes of the market. Then, by analyzing our own and others' experience of this master, a rereading can be proposed that seeks recovery, correction, and expansion of perspective. Through critical reflection on shared findings, in the light of another logic, the gospel's story of who/whose we and others really are can be appropriated. Such a critical process belongs to pastoral theology.

Dialectical Ingredients

When examined as a pastoral context for faith development, the current reality of prevailing economic insecurity is one that calls for affirmative action, on behalf of both oneself and others. This can take a self-critical form, of faith redevelopment through reflective analysis of patterns that have functioned to underdevelop persons and communities, both materially and spiritually. I use the terms, "develop," "underdevelop," and "redevelop," in a conscious effort to make a conceptual connection between faith dynamics and economic processes. This is prompted by Walter Rodney's analysis, *How Europe Underdeveloped Africa,* in which he constructs the term "underdevelop" as an active verb. In this sense, I argue that the faith that functioned to legitimate the economic underdeveloping of Africa, served to produce in the sponsors/perpetrators of "Christian mission" a phenomenon of underdeveloped, i.e., uncritical, faith. On the part of receivers and/or victims of that mission, however, resources of resilient, critical faith have emerged. My diagnosis of underdeveloped faith in the so-called developed world, and my identification of resources for faith redevelopment in the so-called underdeveloped world, are derived from Rodney's understanding of development. In response to the question, "What is development?", his introductory definitional response is one that informs my discussion of faith development/redevelopment. It speaks relevantly to a social context where the socioeconomic infrastructure is being

91

rapidly *underdeveloped,* through economic, political, and cultural triage:

> Development in human society is a many-sided process. At the level of the individual, it implies increased skill and capacity, greater freedom, creativity, self-discipline, responsibility and material well-being. Some of these are virtually moral categories and are difficult to evaluate — depending as they do on the age in which one lives, one's class origins, and one's personal code of what is right and what is wrong. However, what is indisputable is that the achievement of any of those aspects of personal development is very much tied in with the state of the society as a whole. From earliest times, [humanity] found it convenient and necessary to come together in groups to hunt and for the sake of survival. The relations which develop within any given social group are crucial to an understanding of the society as a whole. . . . At the level of social groups, therefore, development implies an increasing capacity to regulate both internal and external relationships.[2]

I have already identified historical dimensions of active developing/underdeveloping. I have proposed an interrogation of received schooling, to identify gaps, distortions, and euphemistic versions of the past. A recovery/discovery of dissonant voices and/or subjugated traditions can provide hermeneutical resources. They provide tools for understanding and evaluating congruence or incongruence between traditional truth claims, our own and others' experience. Communal dialectical activity generates conscious experience of both liberation and captivity. New meanings arise from critical human encounters. Personal or vicarious experiences alter previous understandings of human limits and divine power. The good news/bad news tension of this experience is heightened in the current context of prevailing dehumanization. Diverse experiences of contradiction, dissonance, ambiguity, anxiety, resistance, and eschatological hope have been variously expressed. For example:

2. Walter Rodney, *How Europe Underdeveloped Africa* (Harare, Zimbabwe: Zimbabwe Publishing House, 1972), 9.

Do not adjust your mind, there's a fault in reality. (Anon.)

The world seen clearly is seen through tears. So, why ask me what's wrong with my eyes? (novelist Margaret Atwood)

Don't Mourn, Organize. (Working Peoples Alliance, Guyana)

First Mourn
Then work for change. (Memorial, "Montreal Massacre")

'Twas grace that taught my heart to fear,
And grace my fears relieved. ("Amazing Grace," John Newton)

Knowing Voices

The voices selected here and proposed as resources for critical faith development/redevelopment are those reflecting dialectical ingredients of "knowing" that can be redemptive. First, there are voices that convey knowing that something is wrong, knowing what can and must be changed, and knowing what the costs will be. The following two voices, one citing the other, articulate a cumulative tradition of critical awareness concerning the costly processes of colonization and subsequent decolonization of the Third World.

Voices: Cornel West, Professor of Religion and Afro-American Studies, and Frantz Fanon, Algerian revolutionary

> Born of violent struggle, consciousness-raising and the reconstruction of identities, decolonization simultaneously brings with it new perspectives on that long-festering underside of the Age of Europe (of which colonial domination represents the *costs* of "progress," "order" and "culture"), as well as requiring new readings of the economic boom in the USA (wherein the black, brown, yellow, red, female, elderly, gay, lesbian, and white working class live the same *costs* as cheap labor at home in addition to US-dominated Latin American and Pacific Rim markets).

The impetuous ferocity and moral outrage that motors the decolonization process is best captured by Frantz Fanon in *The Wretched of the Earth* (1961):

> In decolonization, there is therefore the need of complete calling into question of the colonial situation. If we wish to describe it precisely, we might find it in the well-known words: "The first shall be last and the last first." Decolonization is the putting into practice of this sentence. The naked truth of decolonization evokes for us the searing bullets and blood-stained knives which emanate from it. For the last to be first, this will only come to pass after a murderous and decisive struggle between the two protagonists [native and settler].[3]

The conflictual dynamics of reversal in Fanon's conviction raise obvious questions as to how such knowing can be redeeming for those who are already first, and how it will remain redemptive for the "last" once they have become "first."

There are voices that show how redemptive knowing has particular, concrete content, characterized by knowing who is with, for, or against us, and what allies and resources are needed if the context is to be reformed and/or transformed.

Voice: Eduardo Galeano

> Those who deny liberation to Latin America also deny our only possible rebirth, and incidentally absolve the existing structures from blame. Our youth multiplies, rises, listens: What does the voice of the system offer? The system speaks a surrealist language. In lands that are empty it proposes to avoid births; in countries where capital is plentiful but wasted it suggests that capital is lacking; it describes as "aid" the deforming orthopedics of loans and the draining of wealth that results from foreign investment; it calls upon big landowners to carry our agrarian reforms and upon the oligarchy to practice social justice. . . . Is everything forbidden us except to fold our arms? Poverty is not

3. Cornel West, *Keeping Faith: Philosophy and Race in America* (New York: Routledge, 1993), 12-13.

written in the stars; underdevelopment is not one of God's mysterious designs. Redemptive years of revolution pass; the ruling classes wait and meanwhile pronounce hellfire anathema on everybody. In a sense the right wing is correct in identifying itself with tranquillity and order: it is an order of daily humiliation for the majority, but an order nonetheless; it is a tranquillity in which injustice continues to be unjust and hunger to be hungry. If the future turns out to be a Pandora's box, the conservative has reason to shout, "I have been betrayed." And the ideologists of impotence, the slaves who look at themselves with the master's eyes, are not slow to join in the outcry. . . . Recovery of the resources that have always been usurped is recovery of our destiny.[4]

Finally there are voices that articulate why redemptive knowing involves knowing that *what* we know, or don't know, is connected with who we are. It reflects the concrete circumstances that govern that identity and social location. Such knowing often seems to be grounded in knowing who and whose we are, *in* the actual experience of those circumstances. The following voice from inside the experience of "black religion," articulates the contextualized experiential basis and concrete spirituality of this profound way of knowing. Citing Spencer's discourse at some length provides an interpretive context for my concluding reflection on the redemptive knowing of Marian Wright Edelman, in which marks of anticipation as "hope in action" are identified.

Voice: Jon Michael Spencer, cultural critic, Associate Professor of African and Afro-American Studies

> One day, when Moses had grown up, he went out to his people and looked on their burdens; and he saw an Egyptian beating a Hebrew, one of his people. He looked this way and that, and seeing no one he killed the Egyptian and hid him in the sand. (Exod. 2:11-12)

---

4. Eduardo Galeano, *Open Veins of Latin America: Five Centuries of Pillage of a Continent* (New York and London: Monthly Review Press, 1973), 99.

Moses' killing the Egyptian was "the first blow of liberation from Egypt" [Ernst Bloch]. The ensuing exodus, the type of liberation unattainable by one raised as a slave or by one unconnected with the slaves, was possible only by one brought up in the midst of oppressors and who had been educated in the ways of their wisdom and power. Thereafter, Moses went out to his people and looked on their burdens.

For the enslaved Africans, the first blows of liberation from bondage could only have been brought about by those liberated from a slave mentality — who, being brought up in the midst of oppressors, appropriated the power and wisdom of the gospel. . . .

"Liberation is not simply a history that breaks in from a future totally unconnected with the present," defines Jose Miguez-Bonino. "It is a project which springs from the protest born of the suffering of the present; a protest to which God grants a future in which [humanity] enters through [God's] action." James Cone adds that revelation is "God's self-disclosure to [humanity] *in a situation of liberation.*" Thus the situation of liberation initiated by Moses' first blow of freedom — the time of God's self-revelation is a flame of fire out of the midst of a bush — included God's promise of a future land, which the Israelites would enter by their actions behind the rod of Moses, under the watchful eye of God.

Whether the people of Africa were engaged in actions of insurrection, or exodus, or incessant passages into liberation, or through masked confrontation and conflict, one thing is clearly evident in the spirituals: The enslaved figured out why they should be free — "My Lord delivered Daniel/*and why not every[one]?*" — and the figuring was done in a situation of liberation, commencing with the "middle passage" when some engaged in insurrection and others leaped headlong into the sea just to be free. The spirituals were theological reflections of a long-standing practice of liberation and therefore songs of revelation and liberation.

*   *   *

The spirituals lyricized an inward liberation exhibited in the conversion of Virginia ex-slave George Anderson. Long before the Confederate Army surrendered, Anderson claimed to have found the source of liberation at a camp meeting: "I did not cast off the chains of slavery at the time of the surrender," he said, "they fell off at that camp meeting." Anderson's conversion into the Christian body of liberation was the consequence of anticipation. As Witvliet argues, "The emancipatory longing for liberation is included in the anticipation of a new world in which the last are first. . . . Anticipation is hope in action. . . . When Moses spoke what the Lord said regarding the promise, the people of Africa, with active hope (faith) in Christ, fervently anticipated emancipation and salvation.

> The very time I thought I was lost
> The dungeon shook and the chains fell off.
> You may hinder me here but you cannot there,
> 'Cause God in the heaven going to answer prayer.

The spirituals seem to indicate that the type of conversion Anderson had was a prerequisite to faithfully seeking freedom from bondage, that Christ was the source of *authentic* anticipation and *audacious* emancipatory longing. This is perhaps what Herzog meant when he said that liberation "antecedes and transcends our efforts at self-liberation." . . . "Hush, hush, there's somebody callin' my name" refers to an anticipatory summons (a favor) from Jesus Christ to personhood and inward liberation. . . . Herzog concurs that "confronted with God's liberation in Jesus men [and women] can confess that Jesus encounters them not as a stranger, but as one who gives them true identity: he calls them by name — by their true selfhood."

> My Lord calls me.
> He calls me by the thunder,
> The trumpet sounds in my soul. . . .

The autobiographical narratives of Frederick Douglass and Thomas Wentworth Higginson refute the claims that Africans failed to create a body of songs on their enslaved condition. In his *My Bondage and My Freedom* (1855), Douglass gave this illustration:

> A keen observer might have detected in our repeated singing of "O Canaan, sweet Canaan, / I am bound for the land of

Canaan," something more than a hope of reaching heaven. We meant to reach the *north* — and the north was our Canaan.

In the lips of some, it meant the expectation of a speedy summons to a world of spirits; but on the lips of *our* community, it simply meant a speedy pilgrimage toward a free state, and deliverance from all the evils and dangers of slavery.

Thomas Wentworth Higginson, in his *Army Life in a Black Regiment* (1869), told about the outbreak of the civil war when enslaved blacks of Georgetown, South Carolina, were chanting the old spiritual, "We'll soon be free /. . . When the Lord will call us home." A little drummer boy confided in him, said Higginson, that "Dey tink *de Lord* mean for to say *De Yankees*." Cone offers one last retort:

Seeking to detract from the theological significance of the spirituals, some critics may point out that black slaves were literalists in their interpretation of the scripture. . . . But the critical point is that their very literalism supported a black gospel of earthly freedom. They were literal when they sang about Daniel in the lions' den, David and Goliath, and Samson and the Philistines.

The people of Africa were literal in their interpretations of the Old Testament liberation stories. However, the pharaohs of the African slave trade (and their contemporary disciples . . .) projected the David and Samson types into the New Testament — interpreting the Old Testament liberation situations with a Pauline epistemology, an otherworldly rather than empirical eschatology. The scholars who examined the black spirituals with the pharaonic interpretation turned deaf ears and blind eyes to third- and fourth-generation children. These scholars did not listen to or see the solemn warnings, signs, and wonders of the Lord.

$$* \qquad * \qquad *$$

Christ *the Promise* has promised a promised land (John 14:2-3). It is Canaan, the promised land Moses promised projected into eternity. Because it is a land that is always coming — disallowing any flesh to claim, "Alas it is here" — liberation is best understood as a process of maturation. . . . For the people of Africa the ongoing process of ever-increasing freedom was distilled in the image of "climbing Jacob's ladder."[5]

Conversion Dynamics

In the foregoing, dynamics of conversion are discernible as ingredients in faith experience that is testified to as a source of new knowing or knowing better. In "Billy Graham and the Nature of Conversion: A Paradigm Case," John G. Stackhouse, Jr. identifies the prevalent idea of "a variety of conversion trajectories, with some centering on particular *crisis* experience and others characterized by a *process* of growing acquaintance with and trust in Jesus Christ."[6] Claiming Billy Graham as belonging to the latter category, Stackhouse provides some criteria for discussing conversion dynamics in a critical theological process of faith redevelopment:

> The Christian life is one of process punctuated by crisis, and the pattern of process and crisis will vary with the individual. Each Christian, though, is in a new life after being born again, and the point is to live that new life not to rest on some past experience, however dramatic. Graham, that is, does not preach what theologian Dietrich Bonhoeffer memorably castigated as "cheap grace": he stands in the classical evangelical tradition of challenging professed Christians to go on in daily, growing obedience to Christ. . . . Graham stands in the venerable tradition of the revival. For revival strictly speaking can only come to those already alive, and that means, in this understanding, simply stirring up the already-converted to new spiritual vigour . . . Graham is not uninterested politically . . . [he] concentrates on what he continues to believe is the only lasting solution to macro as well as micro problems, the one-by-one conversion of men and women to new life in Christ.[7]

5. Jon Michael Spencer, *Protest and Praise: Sacred Music of Black Religion* (Minneapolis: Fortress Press, 1990).

6. John G. Stackhouse, Jr., "Billy Graham and the Nature of Conversion: A Paradigm Case," *Studies in Religion/Sciences Religieuses* 21:3 (1992): 339.

7. Ibid., 343.

In the context of the "global economy," I define critical faith as faith that is empowered consciously, to apprehend harm in the production of human surplus, and to comprehend such harm as a humanly constructed evil. Such critical awareness is grounded in experience. It knows that God's intention for creation is *not* the reduction of human life to commodification, in which the real lives of real persons can become surplus commodities. Redeveloped faith, i.e., revival of the already converted to spiritual vigor, critically and concretely interpreted, may be observable in what have been defined in social science terms as conversion, alternation, and commitment:

> "Conversion," according to sociologists Irwin Barker and Raymond Currie, "is defined as a radical break with one's former identity such that the past and the present are antithetical in some important respects." "Alternation" is "a transition in which a new identity develops naturally out of the old one." . . . And "commitment" is measured by the intellectual, experiential and practical ways in which one's "adhesion" to the new identity manifests itself.[8]

In conversion, alternation, and commitment, the actualization of critical faith or redemptive knowing, as understood in this study, may or may not be discernible. For me, an important determinant has to do with whether and how coming to critical consciousness (e.g., awareness of race, class, gender, sexual privilege, ethnic history, material resources, etc.) has been a factor in one's changed faith perspective, one's attitudes and behavior. Structural analysis of effects of the "global economy" can be a liberating process if and when discovering who we are or were in the eyes of others, creates a conscious need to know more, to know better. It may compel us to seek out those with whom we can facilitate mutual faith redevelopment as redemptive knowing. This begins with knowing that something is wrong and knowing enough to recognize a need to know more. It means knowing who and whose we are; knowing who is with/for and against us; knowing which others we

8. Ibid., 348.

need in order to know more. Finally, it involves knowing how to live with what we know, with awareness that what we know now is never all there is.

Social Analysis and Faith Formation

When Good Conscience is Uncritical Faith

Inherent in this study is an operative conviction that mutual empowerment for faith redevelopment requires externalizing what may be internalized blocks to redemptive knowing. Such blocks include fear of dehumanization (one's own and others'), strategies of denial and evasion, and counterfeits of well-being. In order to access or appropriate critical resources for authentic hope, i.e., channels of grace, both "winners" and "losers" in the "global economy" need to address such obstacles. They confound a critical reading of the social reality and thwart or subvert the initiative for a redemptive rereading.

In the tradition of Western Christianity, such psychosocial impediments may be found to be consolidated into a personal or collective sense of good conscience. Here I speak of "good conscience" colloquially and nonclinically. I intend to convey a sense of general self-approbation. By personal, societal, or religious criteria of moral judgment, and in accordance with how one perceives one's power or lack of power to meet those standards, one is "okay," one "feels good" about oneself. The notion of good conscience as uncritical consciousness, and the exploring of a process of critical reconstruction of good conscience are pursued here in terms of faith redevelopment. Some working parameters are suggested by Paul Lehmann's critical orientation in *Ethics in a Christian Context*:

> The decisive question of ethics [is] what it really takes to make and keep human life human. What it really takes is nothing other than a firm foundation for setting the conscience of [people] forever, not at rest, but free. . . .
>
> . . . The semantic, philosophical and theological pilgrimage of

101

conscience begins with the Greek tragedians of the fifth century before Christ and ends with Sigmund Freud. It is a moving, tortuous record of decline and fall which forces upon us in our time the frankest possible facing of a sharp alternative: either "do the conscience over" or "do the conscience in!" Ethical theory must either dispose of the conscience altogether or completely transform the interpretation of its ethical nature, function, and significance.[9]

I explore here the latter of Lehmann's alternatives, i.e., the transformative option. Can good conscience function as an agent of, rather than a block to, redemptive knowing, through the integration of social analysis and theological reflection? Lehmann's concept of *conscience-relation* is relevant theory for an exploration of re-evangelization and conscientization, through critical pastoral dialogue between "winners" and "losers" in the "global economy":

> The ethical significance and function of my neighbor's conscience are concretely exhibited in the *conscience-relation* between my neighbor and myself. This *conscience-relation* is a relation of human claim and human response through which no human action is ethical in itself but all human action is instrumental to what God in Christ is doing in the world to make and keep life human.[10]

His emphasis on the context of conscience calls for critical pastoral theology that can empower the discernment of dehumanization and animate rehumanizing faith responses:

> Luther began his theological career at Wittenberg with a course of lectures on the Psalms. There — in that inexhaustible treasury of Old Testament piety — he came upon the interchangeability of conscience and heart. . . . Luther [as Paul] perceived the validating context of conscience and to this extent set the conscience free for its obedient ministry of humanization.[11]

9. Paul Lehmann, *Ethics in a Christian Context* (New York: Harper and Row, 1963), 327.
10. Ibid., 360.
11. Ibid., 363, 365.

Good conscience, as a social construct, may function as false consciousness or uncritical faith. It may constitute an effective and/or affective barrier to consciously experiencing a relation of human claim and human response. This blocks any conscious experience of a *need* for new knowing. As an impediment to critical awareness of conscience-relation, what *is* this ideological/psychological phenomenon of good conscience? For a characteristic but limited profile, I refer briefly to three interpreters of cognate secular knowledge. Robert Lifton's insights are informed by social history, psychology, and psychiatry; Michael Lerner's by philosophy and clinical psychology; and Lillian B. Rubin's by sociology and psychotherapy. In these Jewish voices I discern an integrative spirit in which social analysis and the dynamics of faith formation, reformation, and transformation combine to provide illumination for the integrative discipline of pastoral theology.

Integrating Death Equivalents

In both North and South, the "global economy" functions to actualize a kind of living death (cynicism, hopelessness, hardness of heart) in which the humanness of human life is destabilized. A hostile economic spirit prevails. The need to consume or be consumed, to compete profitably or die, undermines and destroys the value of human persons and communities. In *The Protean Self: Human Resilience in an Age of Fragmentation*, Robert J. Lifton exposes human responses to such effects. For Christians in the North, internalized awareness of what Pobee calls "worship of the free market and the death of the poor," can be experienced as a sense of complicity and structural/ideological captivity. This is analagous to what Lifton describes as "death equivalents." From the characteristics of Proteus, a god in Greek mythology, he derives the concept of "proteanism" to describe the ethos of the survivor, and a human capacity to transcend living death by changing shape in response to crisis. The following citation documents insights from Lifton that illumine for me the critical task of theology in developing theory and practice for pastoral care, in the fragmenting context of "globalization":

Death and renewal — the self as survivor — is, for proteanism both metaphor and psychological principle. A survivor is one who has encountered death, literally or figuratively — one who has witnessed and been touched by it — while remaining alive. Over the twentieth century, human beings have survived extremities of not only mass killing and dying but also spiritual assault and dislocation. Either way, survivors are haunted by death, not only its actuality but by immediate death equivalents . . . feelings of separation (from nurturing communities, individuals and principles), of disintegration (of falling apart or fearing that one will), and of stasis (of being stymied, static, immobilised). At the ultimate level, one may feel divested of larger connectedness, of the various modes of symbolic immortality. Pervasive in all these feelings is a sense of loss. . . . The ethos of the survivor can also contribute to reconstituting the self in the face of that loss.[12]

In the experience of the survivor, Lifton finds patterns that are both problematic and a possible source of learning something: e.g., "death imprints" as knowledge informing commitment to life enhancement; "death guilt" as a source of heightened ethical consciousness; "psychic numbing" as potentially positive adapting skill; "suspicion of counterfeit nurturance" as a sharpened sense of inauthenticity; "struggle for meaning" as motivation for mission. In all of these patterns, criteria can be discerned for a critical reappropriation of the symbolic power of Christian acts of ministry. They can actualize meanings that reconstitute persons as whole, as made in the image of God. Lifton finds what he calls "the principle of commonality," important for "species awareness," as a resource for surviving loss of meaning and human connection:

We assert our commonality through our capacity for empathy, for thinking and feeling our way into the mind of others. In allowing us to "resonate" with other people, "experiencing their experience," empathy is a key to species awareness. . . . Empathy is to be distinguished from sympathy . . . and from identifica-

12. Robert J. Lifton, *The Protean Self: Human Resilience in an Age of Fragmentation* (New York: Basic Books, 1993), 81.

tion. . . . What empathy does require is that one include the other's humanity in one's own imagination. . . . There is . . . an evolution of a "natural psychology" which provides "every member of the human species both the power and the inclination to use a privileged picture of his [or her] own self as a model for what it is like to be another person."[13]

Denial and Investment in Powerlessness

As testified to in previously cited voices, e.g., Tamez and Spencer, the faith experience of Christians has been externalized and articulated as a process of mutual recognition, of discovering, remembering, and internalizing who/whose they are. This theme of recovery of the ethos and spirit of original identity and commission is the point of departure for Michael Lerner's work, in *Jewish Renewal: A Path to Healing and Transformation:*

> Judaism presents the world with a challenge: that the world can and should be fundamentally changed; that the central task facing the human race is *tikkun olam*, the healing and transformation of the world. And Judaism has deep insight into how that can be accomplished. Yet in every generation, this insight has been muted, avoided, abandoned, or outright denied by many, including those who claim to be the official priests, spokespeople, leaders, rabbis, teachers, or orthodox embodiments of Judaism. Jewish renewal is the process, repeated throughout Jewish history, in which Judaism is "changed" back to its origins as the practice of healing, repair, and transformation.[14]

A relational dynamic is a major premise in Michael Lerner's work:

> Human beings become more fully themselves through a process of mutual recognition, and when that process is stymied it provides angry and sometimes oppressive behavior. God is the force

13. Ibid., 214.
14. Michael Lerner, *Jewish Renewal: A Path to Healing and Transformation* (New York: G. P. Putnam's Sons, 1994), p. xvii.

in the universe that makes possible this process of recognition, and part of what is recognized is the God within each of us (namely, the way we are created in the image of God and hence equally worthy of respect and love.) The fears, the accumulated angers and pains, the legacy of cruelty that combine to make it difficult for human beings to recognize one another have been a major source of evil throughout history.[15]

Lerner's concepts of "politics of meaning," "ethos of caring," and "ethically grounded communities" as antidotes to dehumanization are based on a species awareness grounded in Jewish scripture. In the narrative framework of the biblical story, he identifies dynamics of denial and avoidance that function to paralyze apprehension of harm. Such loss of nerve forecloses on any critical process (e.g., structural analysis) that might empower resistance, as a faith response, as comprehension of harm. It preempts anticipation of liberation and produces a refusal to hope:

> Return with me to the moment of revelation, the moment when a people "gets it" that the world can be different, a people that has just experienced something that turned the entire world upside down, showing the inevitability of oppression to be a lie — a moment that subordinates the lawlike regularity of nature to a higher spiritual and moral order. The psalmist can declare that when Israel left Egypt, "the sea saw it and fled, the mountains danced like rams, the little hills like young sheep" (Psalm 114:2-3). They have personally experienced the fundamental truth of the universe: the possibility of possibility. They are overwhelmed by it, excited by it, and momentarily they understand that they have to embody this understanding in how they treat one another, in the way they conduct their lives, and they must tell this message to others, teach it to their children, shout and rejoice about it.
>
> Yet it is only a moment later that they get scared. It's too much, the burden of this knowledge. And so they want to retreat from it, go back to Egypt, or at least recast their lives as loyal

15. Ibid., xx.

children of Egypt, dancing around the golden calf and doing their best to recreate a relationship to gods with which they are familiar. They are not people who have lost religion — they still have the consciousness, shared by other nations, that the world deserves to be celebrated. But they have lost the memory that the God that created the world is also the God that makes the transformation possible. According to the Torah account, God's first reaction is anger. Perhaps this people should be replaced. But eventually a different response emerges. Urged by Moses to reconsider, God establishes the other side of His/Her being, the side of compassion.[16]

In my inquiry, I am trying to identify obstacles to critically redeveloped faith responses to the global phenomenon of the production of human surplus. Insightful for this exploration is Lerner's concept of "surplus powerlessness." It functions to block apprehension, comprehension, and visualization of harm that would call for social change, in anticipation of liberation:

> Even when external oppression is gone and human beings appear free to act in accord with their highest selves, they still face the debilitating psychological effects of oppression and the internalization of cruelty. There is more than real powerlessness standing in the way of human improvement. There is also what I call surplus powerlessness, the degree to which individuals have internalized their powerlessness and become convinced that the way things are now is the only way they can be. . . . In every historical period there is a thickly embroidered set of ideas that are described as "common sense," which are in fact the summary set of expressions by which people reassure one another that what is is all that could be, and that one is foolish to try anything else. In most historical periods, this common sense is also dressed up in more formal garb — in the form of religious, metaphysical (or in the latest incarnation) scientific beliefs that serve to reinforce this deep conviction that nothing much can be changed.

16. Ibid., 110-11.

But surplus powerlessness is not just some set of ideas about the world — it is also intertwined with a complex set of feelings about oneself. Most human beings are deeply committed to the picture they have of themselves as beings who do not really deserve to be more loved, more free, more joyous, or more fulfilled than they actually are. They have an internalized picture of themselves as the kinds of persons who deserve whatever happens to them. . . . Sinai is a moment of dramatic illumination. But when one comes down from such a moment, the life we lead takes over, and things do not change automatically because illumination has happened. The deep structuring of surplus powerlessness makes the patterns of distorted consciousness embedded in the institutions and social practices difficult to dislodge.[17]

Dispelling Myths

As a sociologist and psychotherapist, Lillian Rubin's critical consciousness is informed by social research that she began to see as a collaborative process:

The research seemed like a collaboration, since I learned from the people I spoke with what I had not known to ask and then incorporated it into the study, making it richer, more complex, and, I hope, more true to the fact and spirit of their lives.[18]

Her work provides framework for understanding the apparent resilience of good conscience in the face of disconfirming evidence that all is not as it should be. Studying the responses of working-class Americans she affirms their prevailing "cry from the heart" that "it's not fair." Rubin acknowledges the grim reality of structured economic disparities and asks:

17. Ibid., 111-12.
18. Lillian B. Rubin, *Families on the Faultline: America's Working Class Speaks About the Family, the Economy, Race, and Ethnicity* (New York: HarperCollins, 1984), 25.

How it is that our national discourse continues to focus on the middle class, denying the existence of a working class and rendering them invisible?[19]

Her explanation serves my inquiry into the dynamics and potential of critical faith redevelopment, i.e., faith formation incorporating social analysis, for empowering resistance against dehumanization:

> Whether a family or a nation, we all have myths that play tag with reality — myths that frame our thoughts, structure our beliefs, and organize our systems of denial. A myth encircles reality, encapsulates it, controls it. It allows us to know some things and to avoid knowing others, even when somewhere deep inside we really know that we don't want to know. Every parent has experienced this clash between myth and reality. We see signals that tell us a child is lying and explain them away. It isn't that we can't know; it's that we won't, that knowing is too difficult or painful, too discordant with the myth that defines the relationship, the one that says: *My child wouldn't lie to me.*
>
> The same is true about a nation and its citizens. Myths are part of our national heritage, giving definition to the national character, offering guidance for both public and private behavior, comforting us in our moments of doubt. Not infrequently our myths trip over each other, providing a window into our often contradictory and ambivalently held beliefs. The myth that we are a nation of equals lives side-by-side in these United States with the belief in white supremacy. And, unlikely as it seems, it's quite possible to believe both at the same time. Sometimes we manage the conflict by shifting from one side to the other. More often, we simply redefine reality. The inequality of condition between whites and blacks isn't born in prejudice and discrimination, we insist; it's black inferiority which is the problem. Class distinctions have nothing to do with privilege, we say; it's merit that makes the difference.[20]

The social myth-making phenomenon which Rubin identifies is important for any Christian faith redevelopment project. It has

19. Ibid., 93.
20. Ibid., 239.

particular relevance for the task of reconstituting *all* persons as *humans*, made in the image of God. Critical faith formation integrates structural analysis and personal reflection. It can focus on where and how constructions of whiteness/blackness, femininity/masculinity, heterosexuality/homosexuality, etc. promote and sustain social alienation. Alienated relations contaminate possibilities for theologically rereading human interactions. They inhibit discernment of what Pobee refers to as "the encounter with and experience of the human face of God in the contemporary world." Rubin provides an analytical basis for understanding why, in the absence of such Christian or other humanizing encounters, the socially constructed "public and psychological wages" of whiteness can function to entrench economic costs and benefits, not only along racial lines but also according to class, gender, and ethnicity:

> Along with the importation of an immigrant population, the separation of black and white workers has given American capital a reserve labor force to call upon whenever white workers seemed to them to get too "uppity." Thus, while racist ideology enables white workers to maintain their belief in their superiority, they have paid for that conviction by becoming far more vulnerable in the struggle for decent wages and working conditions than they might otherwise have been. Politically and economically, the ideology of white supremacy disables white workers from making the kind of interracial alliances that would benefit all of the working class. Psychologically, it leaves them exposed to the double-edged sword. . . . On one side, their belief in the superiority of whiteness helps to reassure them that they are not at the bottom of the social hierarchy. But their insistence that their achievements are based on their special capacities and virtues, that it's only incompetence that keeps others from grabbing a piece of the American dream, threatens their precarious sense of self-esteem. For if they're the superior ones, the deserving ones, the ones who earned their place solely through hard work and merit, there's nothing left but to blame themselves for their inadequacies when hard times strike. . . . As the economy continues to falter, and local, state, and federal governments keep cutting services, there are more and more acrimonious debates

about who will share in the shrinking pie. Racial and ethnic groups, each in their own corners, square off as they ready themselves for what seems to be the fight of their lives. Meanwhile, the quality of life for all but the wealthiest Americans is spiralling downward — a plunge that's felt most deeply by those at the lower end of the class spectrum, regardless of color.[21]

I have already alluded to this economic, psychosocial phenomenon. It is discernible in the threatened identity and security of Canadians of white Anglo-Saxon descent. The changing demographic makeup of Canada challenges our historical sense of entitlement and cultural hegemony. The dehumanization of "losers" *and* "winners" in the "global economy" deepens through normalizing the exclusion of those at the bottom of the social order. Faith is and remains underdeveloped through clinging to social mythology (and debased anthropology) which blames the poor and validates economic, political, and cultural triage. Both of these tendencies can function with a sense of good conscience. Uncritical personal faith guards against unwelcome learning experiences. This conditions collective collusion in uncritical communal faith practices which raise no awkward questions for those who "know enough to know that they don't want to know any more."[22] By means of illusionary assurances that "what you don't know won't hurt you," or, "we're better off not knowing," not-knowing is constructed as innocence.

Rubin compares her current findings with the results of research she conducted twenty years ago: "In the opening sentences of *Worlds of Pain* I wrote that America was choking on its differences. If we were choking then, we're being asphyxiated now."[23] Here Rubin refers to her previous work, *Worlds of Pain: Life in the Working-Class Family:*

21. Ibid., 243-44.
22. "The people in the Third Reich knew enough to know that they did not want to know any more," reported by Martin Rumscheidt, from personal conversation with Eberhard Bethge, friend and biographer of Dietrich Bonhoeffer.
23. Rubin, *Families on the Faultline*, 244.

When the smoke and dust of the sixties had settled, America rediscovered class, race, and ethnicity. A century after the great waves of immigration, more than seventy-five years after settlement houses and public schools undertook to "civilize" and assimilate the immigrants' children, and decades after social scientists celebrated the melting pot and wrote glowingly of our ultimate triumph — the disappearance of class distinctions and antagonisms — America choked on its differences.[24]

Rubin notes the disappearance of a belief once prevalent among working-class Americans, that personal sacrifice and hard work is the key and guarantee for progress in America. More important for Christian existence, especially in the current economic and pastoral context, is Rubin's estimation of what is at stake, in lowered expectations and confidence, in heightened fear, anxiety, and despair. Her analysis represents a daunting challenge for the formation and critical reconstruction of Christian conscience and its ministry of humanization. Rubin's conclusions provoke apprehension *and* comprehension of harm, the critical dynamics which belong to rereading social reality. This is a critical theological process of humanization and rehumanization. It is a redemptive process that begins by dismantling internal supports for denial of harm, through mutual disclosure of the *effects* of harm. Such sharing of life experience provides an interpersonal cost-benefit analysis of counterfeit success dreams and the strategies of entrepreneurial individualism. Illusions of self-determination, personal autonomy, consumer choice, etc. are tested and challenged. Can the gospel context of conscience-relation, of human claim and human response, provide space for such critical encounter?

For me, Rubin identifies indispensable, dialogical elements of *rereading*. This makes re-visioning the social context an urgent and possible communal project:

> The innocence is gone. But is this a cause for mourning?
> Perhaps only when innocence is gone and our eyes unveiled

---

24. Lillian B. Rubin, *Worlds of Pain: Life in the Working-Class Family* (New York: Basic Books, Inc. Publishers, 1976), 3.

will we be able to grasp fully the depth of our conflicts and the sources from which they spring.

We live in difficult and dangerous times, in a country deeply divided by class, race, and social philosophy. The pain with which so many American families are living today, and the anger they feel, won't be alleviated by a retreat to false optimism and easy assurances. Only when we are willing to see and reckon with the magnitude of our nation's problems and our people's suffering, only when we take in the full measure of that reality, will we be able to find the path to change. Until then, all our attempts at solutions will fail. And this, ultimately, will be the real cause for mourning. For without substantial change in both our public and our private worlds, it is not just the future of the family that is imperiled but the very life of the nation itself.[25]

Critical dialectical dynamics such as these have arrested past communities of Christians, animated them, and produced empowering moments of *kairos*. In such moments of crisis and possibility, where room is made for grace, both fear and hope are palpable. I believe this can happen again.

Theological Rereading

Saving Content

All of these discoveries reveal consequences to reading the context of the "global economy" as one in which evil is manifested as dehumanization. A theological rereading depends upon finding criteria for re-visioning the context as redeemed, Such criteria need to be grounded in experience of the possibility of its being rehumanized. A theological rereading gathers elements of what can be recovered or discovered to ground critical faith. It proclaims a definition of humanness which consciously reclaims persons in a context that it reads as dehumanized. It calculates the value of *all* persons as that of humans made in the image of God, and loved

25. Rubin, *Families on the Faultline*, 247.

113

by God. This is the concrete theological content that I designate as saving content.

A theological rereading of a dehumanizing social context articulates saving faith content as the grounds for re-visioning that context. It is able to provide a rationale for denouncing what is proclaimed inevitable. It can account for the authority by which it announces what is possible. The critical re-evangelizing dynamics of such a rereading are discernible in the following reflective analysis from James Dunning:

> Listen to the messages from Madisonavenueland about salvation: Datsun saves. K-Mart is your saving place. Buick is something to believe in. GE brings good things to life. How to wrap your package? — Warner's Bra. A heart to heart talk with Climatrol Computer. Coke is the real thing. Love is Musk. . . . Even though Gallup claims that ninety percent of us believe in God, who is the American God? How much of this is what Robert Bellah calls a "civil religion," not releasing energies in society for the reign of God but harnessing the Gospel for the American way? As Calvin Coolidge said, the American way means that the business of America is business. Do Jesus and the reign of God drive business toward salvation, or do Datsun and Buick drive Jesus? . . . In a narcissistic time conversion can mean born-again in Jesus, preaching Jesus but not the kingdom of justice and freedom which he preached. Jim Wallis writes: "By neglecting the kingdom of God in our preaching, we have lost the integrating and central core of the gospel. The disastrous result is 'saved' individuals who comfortably fit into the old order while the new order goes unannounced." . . . Our own country was founded with a vibrant biblical faith that envisioned our founding mothers and fathers as a new people of God, on exodus into a new promised land which offered liberty and justice for all in a new covenant between God and the people. That vision has brought freedom and untold blessings for millions of people. It has not meant liberty and justice for all. We founded this nation on broken promises to the original inhabitants of this great land. The Revolutionary period granted rights only to white, male land-owners. The Civil War sought to extend those rights beyond

the white middle-class. Robert Bellah claims that our own times clamor for Americans to smash the idols of nationalism and extend those blessings beyond our national boundaries.[26]

Recovery/Discovery of Critical Faith

In order to establish criteria for proposing the possibility of re-humanizing a dehumanized context, I return to Rubenstein's analysis of the production of surplus people. In Rubenstein's work Styron sees a rereading of the meaning of Auschwitz. It reinterprets this event "from the standpoint of its existence as part of a continuum of slavery that has been engrafted for centuries onto the very body of Western civilization."[27] In the light of my discussion of Christian entanglement in imperial culture, I extend this meaning. Inasmuch as Western civilization has been identified as "Christian civilization," such engrafting of slavery has also functioned historically to compromise the Christian church as the Body of Christ. Styron diagnoses Rubenstein's linkage of the (legal) institution of slavery with the (legal) mass murder and mass slavery of Auschwitz as "the sleeping virus in the bloodstream of civilization."[28] Styron reads what has been read as "a diabolical, perhaps freakish excrescence." Then he rereads it as coextensive with, but exceeding the scope of, any previous utilization of human life "in terms of its simple expendability":

> Rubenstein explains in his persuasive first chapter that it is this factor of expendability — an expendability that in turn derives from modern attitudes toward the stateless, the uprooted and rootless, the disadvantaged and dispossessed — that provides still another essential key to the incomprehensible dungeon of

26. James Dunning, "Confronting the Demons: The Social Dimensions of Conversion," in *Conversion and the Catechumenate*, ed. Robert Duggan (New York: Paulist Press, 1984), 27, 33, 36.
27. Richard L. Rubenstein, *The Cunning of History: The Holocaust and the American Future* (New York: Harper and Row, 1978), ix.
28. Ibid., x.

Auschwitz. The matter of surplus populations, which Rubenstein touches upon again and again, haunts this book like the shadow of a thundercloud.[29]

In the dehumanizing logic of the "global economy," the triage factor functions to rationalize human expendability. Therefore, I believe that it is a socioeconomic expedient that carries the "virus" identified by Styron. An antidote must be identified if re-visioning the global context as rehumanized is to be seriously proposed. Any faith content that claims to be saving, needs to integrate critical analysis that will function concretely, as an antidote to the virus of economic, political, and cultural triage. The antidote is for a treatable condition of social pathology. Its symptoms are manifest where some persons, commended as rational, realistic, and/or responsible, can legally, profitably, and in good conscience render other persons expendable. They need only designate such persons unmarketable, surplus, and/or irresponsible. Like Rubenstein's rereading of Auschwitz, saving faith content needs to engage "the painful task of anatomizing the reality within the nightmare while the dream is still fresh."[30]

An Oxford dictionary entry for "antidote" defines the term as, "a medicine given to counteract the influence of poison or an attack of disease." A relevant example is provided: "The whole truth is the best antidote against falsehoods which are dangerous chiefly because they are half-truths." This example implies how the virus manifested in triage may be carried. It spreads through denial of our history of legally destroying surplus or inconveniently situated populations, by rationalizing and spiritualizing their expendability. Therefore, the antidote must effect a critical process of reinterpretation and demystification. It is possible to reread current human disposal strategies, not as inevitable, but as symptomatic of a treatable disease, the course of which is reversible. It requires eyes trained to see events as humanly constructed, often through choices executed on the basis of expediency. Alternative options,

29. Ibid., xi.
30. Ibid., viii.

perhaps previously discounted or defeated, can be recovered or discovered. The discernment and appropriation of theological rationale for such options may provide resources for critically redeveloping faith. The saving content of critical faith witness can ground the task of re-visioning a ministry of humanization in the pastoral context of the "global economy." In *Memory of Fire: Genesis,* Eduardo Galeano voices the intent of such witness:

> They taught us about the past so that we should resign ourselves with drained consciences to the present: not to make history, which was already made, but to accept it. Poor history had stopped breathing: betrayed in academic texts, lied about in classrooms, drowned in dates, they had imprisoned her, with floral wreaths, beneath statuary bronze and monumental marble. Perhaps *Memory of Fire* can help give her back breath, liberty and the word.[31]

In the preface of the North American edition of *The Amnesty of Grace,* the saving content of Elsa Tamez's critical faith witness includes both diagnosis of and antidote for the virus of triage:

> The point of departure for this book is a context of poverty and exclusion. Since, however, the world is structurally united, the structure of sin that gives rise to poverty and exclusion is present in relationships between North and South, and also within the societies of both regions. We thus find throughout the whole world persons who are excluded, as well as others who are responsible for — or at least accomplices in — producing those victims.
>
> We are all both victims and accomplices in the logic of our present-day society, which produces persons who are excluded in all arenas of life: economic, political, social, cultural, and religious. The excluded include those who are poor, women, indigenous peoples, Blacks, persons with physical disabilities, Hispanics and Latinos, Asians — finally all persons whose human worth is negated by society's logic of alienation. They are seg-

31. Eduardo Galeano, *Memory of Fire: Genesis* (New York: Pantheon Books, 1985), xv.

ments of the population who, according to the norms of the society, lack the credentials for acceptance. The law of exclusion that governs our context allows no room for grace. People who are excluded can be called "outcasts" — dispensable and even disposable people.

This logic seems inevitable. It is like the law that enslaves and alienates the consciousness of human beings. They are condemned not to choose for themselves a logic guided by the Spirit of life, which leads to justice and peace.

In this context, Paul's message of the justice of God realized in the justification by faith shines like a ray of dawn's light pushing back the darkness. This message speaks to us of the feasibility of a new logic guided by the power of faith and grace, in opposition to the law that kills and excludes. Jesus Christ lived this life of faith and was the first of many to be justified. Can we believe in what seems impossible in our society, which is based on competition and "thingification" — treating persons like things? Can we believe in a logic of grace and not of merits? If we believe that God raised from the dead the innocent crucified one — the excluded person par excellence — we might be able to trust in a new logic of life in which the law is not imposed from above, in opposition to the worthy life of human beings. Instead, by this new logic we recognize them as persons who have been rendered worthy through the justice of God, so that they can choose their own history, guided by the power of the Spirit.

Even though this study has arisen in a context of exclusion, oppression, and poverty, its message is for everyone. The North American people can be deeply touched, not only because of the foreign policy of their country, which at present is shaped by the exclusionary laws of the neo-liberal market system, but also because they recognize the same logic of exclusion operating on other continents as well. It is evident that in North American society, as in many others, merits are a condition *sine qua non* for being considered a person.

My hope is that we will approach justification by faith without the burden of confessional debates that are often quite futile. Let us go beyond the discussion centered on the disjuncture between faith and works. For our world and our society need the concrete revelation of the justice of God, in a history of sin, plagued by injustices. All of us, sons and daughters of God, are the protagonists of God's justice. The whole creation trembles, says Paul, eagerly awaiting the revelation of the daughters and sons of God.[32]

Discernible in these two voices are the critical dynamics of faith development being explored in this study. They include underdevelopment/redevelopment, recovery/discovery, reading/rereading, apprehension/comprehension of harm, and re-visioning/re-evangelizing. In each case, words are cited from the author's preface to a synthesis of his/her own research. Both voices invite the critical engagement of dialogue partners and anticipate from their readers a committed response. I believe that they mediate critical faith content for integrating social analysis, theological reflection, and spiritual discernment. This can inform the activity of pastoral theology in which theory and practice for the ministry of care is developed.

· In seeking to resuscitate and animate "history," Galeano provides a potential source of new life for "drained consciences." They need to be refilled and watered to their very roots if they are to function to make and keep life human. Graced with life energy and living faith, Tamez reads the global context as dehumanized and rereads it as redeemable through rehumanization. She articulates concrete theological rationale for both readings. This rationale consciously integrates recognition of both the reality of underdeveloped faith and the possibility for critical faith redevelopment as a re-evangelizing process.

In the pastoral context of the "global economy" there is a growing gap between the poles of anxiety/fear and hope. Tamez's concrete understanding of justification as humanization provides a way of bridging what is becoming a rapidly widening gulf. What emerges is a possibility for conversion dynamics in which reading,

32. Elsa Tamez, *The Amnesty of Grace: Justification by Faith from a Latin American Perspective* (Nashville: Abingdon Press, 1993), 7-8.

rereading, and re-visioning facilitate a rebirthing process that makes room for grace. Dehumanized and dehumanizing persons are re-humanized, "born again" as truly *human*, "blessed with the capacity to care for each other here and now."

In my concluding chapter, using elements of case study methodology, I seek to appropriate and integrate the insights of Galeano, Tamez, and other voices introduced in this book. I present a vignette and commentary that project both the real life of real persons and the actual faith of actual people. This provides the medium for demonstrating the relevance of critical faith content for the challenge of re-visioning the context of the "global economy." The vision emerges as *oecumene,* as *new* creation, inhabited by a rehumanized *global* humanity. Introducing the "case" of a black child and her adult advocate, I reread them as "the concrete revelation of the justice of God," which Tamez believes our world and our society need. In the context of a history of black oppression and plagued by racist injustices, these black, female persons can be named "protagonists of God's justice."

CHAPTER FIVE

Re-Visioning the Context

"A Gooder Place"

Vignette for a Case Study

In my neighborhood there is a lot of shooting and three people got shot. On the next day when I was going to school I saw a little stream of blood on the ground. One day after school me and my mother had to dodge bullets. I was not scared.

There is a church and a school that I go to in my neighborhood. There are robbers that live in my building, they broke into our house twice. There are rowhouses in my neighborhood and a man got shot, and he was dead. On another day I saw a boy named Zak get shot. . . . When me and my mother was going to church we could see the fire from the guns being shot in 4414 building. I was not scared. . . .

God is going to come back one day and judge the world. Not just my neighborhood.

I know these are really really bad things, but I have some good things in my neighborhood. Like sometimes my neighborhood is peaceful and quiet and there is no shooting. When me and my mother and some friends go to the lake we have a lot of fun. . . .

I believe in God and I know one day we will be in a gooder place than we are now.[1]

These are the words of eight-year-old Gail. They were quoted in a sermon delivered by Marian Wright Edelman at the National Cathedral in Washington, D.C., on Martin Luther King Day, 1995. This vignette, its rhetorical setting, the personhood of both Gail and Edelman, the hermeneutical context and intended hearers of the sermon, provide the basis for a "case." The "case" integrates ideas presented in an exploration of the implications of the "global economy" for pastoral theology. This approach to integration assumes that vicarious experience of a concrete context can facilitate the appropriation of meanings that matter for faith and faith development. It also claims that there are critical connections between economic contingencies, the dynamics of faith formation, and meanings that matter. These connections function in dialectical tension to produce the critical content of faith knowledge, e.g., "I was not scared . . . I know these are really really bad things. . . . *I believe* in God. . . . *I know* one day we will be in a gooder place."

In using a case study approach to theological integration, I am commending the relevance of theological resources for the ordinary and extraordinary situations of ministry. As part of a comprehensive method of analyzing problems and issues in the church and the world, the "case" can function as a tool for developing a theological understanding of the world. A case scenario can make real the claim that faith is developed and redeveloped in the circumstances of human lives. A case can reveal theological understandings of the world where the dehumanizing circumstances of the real lives of real people shape their actual faith and give it concrete meaning: "God is going to come back and *judge* the *world. Not just my neighborhood.*"

Case study methodology intentionally precipitates and facilitates vicarious experiences. This can produce conflict and heighten personal anxiety. I believe that it is this kind of critical engagement between our own and others' experience that can be a source of

---

1. Marian Wright Edelman, "An Unfinished Symphony: God's Unchanging Call to Heal and Care," *Sojourners* (March/April 1995): 21-22.

formational learning. Such cognitive, spiritual, and theological learning not only opens eyes to new realities but also creates new eyes for seeing assumed realities differently. What is seen through the eyes of faith of those who see anew and see differently is a living theological resource. In the hymn "Amazing Grace," John Newton, a former slave trader, testifies that "I once was blind but now I see." As "living faith of the dead," can such contextualized faith testimony revive the "dead faith of the living?" Can it do so in economic realities where the humanness of human life needs to be reclaimed? Of particular relevance are critical faith dynamics discernible in the witness of those for whom the Christian story is experienced as real. For them, the reality of God in Jesus empowers them to denounce whatever invalidates that story. Such dynamics are evident in the critical encounter between Gail and Marian Wright Edelman, her advocate.

In the following note, *Sojourners,* which printed the sermon in article form, introduces Marian Wright Edelman to readers as

> [the] founder and executive director of the Children's Defense Fund, a national children's advocacy organization in Washington, D.C. . . . CDF coordinates the Black Community Crusade for Children, which has committed itself to "Leave No Child Behind" and to assure every child a healthy, fair, safe, and moral start in life with the support of caring families in nurturing communities.[2]

The rhetorical and theological context in which Gail's words are cited is identified at the outset of Edelman's article, which was entitled "An Unfinished Symphony: God's Unchanging Call to Heal and Care":

> In 1968, Dr. King asked our nation a prescient, urgent, and timely question: Where do we go from here? Chaos or community? In this post-Cold War era of unbearable dissonance between promise and performance, between good politics and good policy, between America's racial creed and America's racial deed, be-

2. Ibid., 23.

tween professed and practiced family values, between calls for community and rampant individualism and greed, and between our capacity to prevent and alleviate child deprivation and disease and our political will to do so, his question demands our 1995 answer with more urgency than ever.

I believe that the overture of our nationhood, the Declaration of Independence, is awaiting its next movement — a movement that is mighty and positive and transforming. A movement which returns us to our founding truths that "All men are created equal" and "are endowed by their creator with certain inalienable rights," among them "life, liberty and the pursuit of happiness."

The ensuing centuries of struggle to extend these truths to women, racial and other minority groups, and children must continue, especially in this time of national moral confusion, family and community breakdown, economic fear and political volatility. If we are going to prevent America's dream and future from becoming a nightmare, we must not sign any new political "contracts" before we review our Old and New Testaments and our American covenant.

God's message through the prophet Zechariah "to see that justice is done, to show kindness and mercy to one another, not to oppress widows, orphans, foreigners who live among you, or anyone else in need" does not change with political fashion. The gospel's injunction, sent into the world by a poor, homeless child Christians call Savior, to bring good rather than bad news to the poor and to set at liberty those who are oppressed, cannot be overruled by political or media pundits anymore than America's enduring values of fairness and opportunity can. God's call to heal and to care is clear and unchanging. Never has that call been more urgent.[3]

It is in a *sermon* that Edelman integrates an analysis of prevailing dehumanization with her critical vision of rehumanizing America's children. Her re-visioning reconstitutes *all* children as real people, created by God for real life, and entitled to live in real hope. In "Gail," all effectively surplus, expendable American children, condemned to

3. Ibid., 21.

"wait in fear," and destined to be "left behind," are found and humanized. This reconstituting process was noted earlier in the "case" of Cielo Toro's work with child miners in Colombia. Both situations manifest a liberation of the conscience for a ministry of humanization. They reveal what is at stake concretely, in the actualization of good conscience and Christian freedom as meanings that matter for real human lives. Paul Lehmann provides an articulation of theological dynamics at work in this redemptive process:

> All things are instrumental to the doing of the will of God as God himself guides and shapes the conscience through the dynamics and the direction of what [God] . . . is doing in the world to make human life human. In marked contrast to behavior done out of respect for [others], conscience is referred to God. Loosed from its dehumanizing context, the conscience is joined instead to the knowledge of good and evil as the environment of humanization. In this context, conscience is nothing other than a good conscience, and a good conscience is nothing other than inward integrity of heart. When the stuff of human behavior is instrumental to such a context of responsibility, the motivational and the structural patterns of humanization may be regarded as taking shape under the fulfilling transformation effected by the politics of God. Bereft of every prescriptive occasion and endowed with the imaginative sensitivity of a good conscience, [persons] behave toward one another on the other side of the ethical predicament, in the confidence that the cleavage between the ethical claim and the ethical act has been overcome by him "from whom and through whom are all things" and "for whom and through whom" they exist. It is from and within the Christian *koinonia* that conscience acquires ethical reality and the power to shape behavior through obedient freedom.[4]

In the sermon which introduces her, Gail is not objectified. Functioning as an individual subject in her own right, she also has a collective identity. Her voice, as presented by Edelman, gives

---

4. Paul Lehmann, *Ethics in a Christian Context* (New York: Harper and Row, 1963), 366.

qualitative substance to statistics which might otherwise function only to quantify harm by cataloguing it:

> Since Dr. King's death, more than one million Americans have been killed violently here at home, including tens of thousands of children. Two hundred seventy-five thousand of them were black. Almost seventeen million children have been born out of wedlock; less than half, eight million, were black. And at least sixteen million babies have been born into poverty, of which four million were black.
>
> An American child is abused or neglected every twenty-six seconds; is born into poverty every half minute; is born to a teen mother every minute; is arrested for a violent crime every five minutes; and is killed by guns every two hours. These shameful numbers have small individual faces and feelings and suffering like that of eight-year-old Gail.

Edelman's commentary on Gail's testimony is cited here to provide context for interpretation and integration with what I have discerned in other voices as critical faith content. Her image of an "unfinished symphony" is noted to convey dynamics of a critical historical consciousness. I cite the conclusion of the sermon to project its invocational and exhortational tone:

> All across our nation, children like Gail are struggling to survive in a living hell, clinging to their faith and their families, and praying that one day they will be in a "gooder place."
>
> In a decent, democratic and moral nation, children shouldn't have to pray and wait in fear. I believe that we are called, as people of faith, to be active participants in working to manifest that "gooder place" right here and now for all of our children.
>
> Can we compose and perform together another great movement of America's unfinished symphony of justice and opportunity? Can you and I act to move our nation back from the brink of violent chaos, racial regression, and class warfare Dr. King warned about? I believe we can.
>
> Abraham Lincoln's Emancipation Proclamation and the thir-

5. Edelman, *Unfinished Symphony*, 21.

126

teenth, fourteenth, and fifteenth Amendments completed the first movement of America's symphony of freedom and justice. Charles Houston, Thurgood Marshall, Dr. Martin Luther King, Jr., Rosa Parks, Fanny Lou Hamer, and thousands of unsung white, brown, and black heroes and heroines, who tore down the walls of legally sanctioned American apartheid, composed the second movement.

Before the new millenium, you and I must and can compose the third movement. We must put social and economic underpinnings beneath the millions of African-American, Asian-American, Latino, white and Native American children left behind when the promise of civil rights laws and the significant progress of the 1960s and '70s in alleviating poverty were eclipsed by the Vietnam War, economic recession, and changing national leadership priorities.

There was real progress. Some things did and do work despite today's political mythology and simplistic, indiscriminate attacks on all social programs. While it is healthy to sort out what works and does not work, it is essential to be specific, careful, and to resist policy by slogan. We are playing politics with human lives.

Let's pray that God's Spirit will be born anew within and among us and help us mount a crusade across our land to stop the killing and neglect of children and heal our racial, class, age, and gender divisions. Every American leader, parent, and citizen must personally and collectively commit to reclaim our nation's soul and give our children back their hope, their sense of security, their belief in America's fairness, and their ability to dream about, envisage, and work toward a future that is attainable and real.[6]

Theology as Faith Response

In her recorded response to the real life and actual faith of an eight-year-old girl, Marian Wright Edelman invokes, in a homiletical context, both the cumulative tradition of the Christian church and the "American covenant." It is here that I appreciate theology as an articulation of an encounter with and experience of the human

6. Ibid., 21-23.

face of God in the contemporary world. What is going on theologically in *this* articulation of encounter? What is being claimed to be
true and saving, or authoritative for human lives? What does it
mean and why does it matter?

Beverly Harrison has articulated what she perceives to be a
critical connection between functioning belief in and response to
God, truth claims made about God, and concrete human contingencies. In her essay, "Theological Reflection in the Struggle for
Liberation: A Feminist Perspective," and under the subheading,
"Learning How to Learn: From Conscientization to Social Analysis," she declares the following:

> Life and death issues are at stake in the way we perceive, analyze,
> and envision the world and therefore in what we say of God and
> human hope. The critical intellectual task of theology is the
> serious one of reappropriating all our social relations, including
> our relations to God, so that shared action toward genuine human
> and cosmic fulfillment occurs.[7]

This assertion, and its theological, rhetorical context, illumines and
is illumined by Edelman's homiletical faith response. It can provide
a hermeneutical key to the critical relationship between the truth
claims Edelman makes, her critical awareness of Gail, and her engagement with the forces that dehumanize American children like Gail.

Dynamics of Critical Faith Response

In Marian Wright Edelman's faith response, the *action* of the *content*
of the Holy Spirit's testimony can be discerned as revelatory, according to the following understanding of revelation: "Faith is not

7. Beverly Wildung Harrison, *Making the Connections: Essays in Feminist
Practice* (Boston: Beacon Press, 1985), 245. Also significant for interpreting
this statement is a contextual note, p. 235: "This essay is an expansion and
revision of two papers delivered originally to international gatherings. I have
retained the framework I used in addressing an academic-based international
audience of political progressives who were also sceptical of feminism."

a once-and-for-all, not a standpoint but a *movement*, the fruit of the Holy Spirit's testimony. It is the action of the content of the testimony which Barth calls the miracle of revelation."[8] This revelatory phenomenon can be discerned in the prayer with which Edelman concludes her sermon:

> Let's pray that God's Spirit will be born anew within and among us and help us mount a crusade across our land to stop the killing and neglect of children and heal our racial, class, age, and gender divisions.

Her reclamation project, "Leave No Child Behind," objectifies and makes concrete a faith response to an experience of salvation. The concrete theological, spiritual *content* of that ongoing faith experience — *her* redemptive knowing, assures Edelman that no living child is unjustifiable, without merit, beyond grace. She apprehends harm in the "facts" of poverty and racism, and comprehends their structural meaning. She *knows* that the expendability of children must be denounced, their status as real people announced and their human credentials validated. She *knows* also, that proactive work to reinstate them into covenantal relationships has begun and needs to be strengthened. Marian Wright Edelman *expects* response. This is an example of anticipation as "hope in action," as cited from Jon Michael Spencer. Her anticipation is the action of the content of revelation. The Holy Spirit's testimony grounds her *continuing* prayer, that God's Spirit *can* be born anew in and among her hearers, and animate them to "leave no child behind." Edelman's faith response also demonstrates the integrated dynamics of "prayer and righteous action," as conceptualized by Dietrich Bonhoeffer and cited in another context by Bärbel von Wartenberg-Potter:

> If the church wants to avoid being a fan-club, or having its truth arise from "cerebral birth," then "prayer and righteous action" must be made to inter-relate in new ways. Eberhard Bethge once interpreted this Bonhoeffer phrase beautifully:

8. H. Martin Rumscheidt, *Revelation and Theology: An Analysis of the Barth-Harnack Correspondence of 1923* (Cambridge: Cambridge University Press, 1972), 147.

> Righteous action among the people saves prayer from becoming an escape into self-satisfied piety. Prayer saves righteous action among the people from self-righteousness. Righteous action saves prayer from the hypocrisy among the pious which the children of the world will never fail to spot. Prayer saves righteous action from the fanatical ideologizing through which those who are committed to change become bad representatives of their own commitment. Righteous action saves prayer from pessimism. Prayer saves righteous action from resignation. Action keeps prayer in the realm of reality; prayer keeps action within the realm of truth.[9]

Through praxis, as a ministry of humanization, the unbearable dissonance Edelman identifies between promise and performance is revealed to be neither absolute nor inevitable. Pastoral agency can then be re-visioned as capable of overruling what Tamez calls the law of exclusion that governs our context, allowing no room for grace.

Edelman responds to both Gail's material existence and the child's belief statement. These critical faith dynamics reinforce my perception of the epistemological significance of the particularity of critical faith content. *Who* one is and *how* one knows, affects and effects *what* one knows — about oneself, others, and God. Edelman's voice is the knowing voice of one who knows who and whose Gail is. And she knows this *in* the experience of dehumanization which Gail experiences as a poor, black, female child in America.

The theological dynamics of integrating meanings that matter, through direct and vicarious experience, is evident in this "case" as Edelman responds to Gail's faith in a "gooder" place. This phenomenon provides a basis for apprehending the critical dynamics of conscientization. This can enable comprehension of a process of redeveloping and nurturing critical faith. It can occur through conscientizing encounter and dialogue, direct and vicarious, between privileged and oppressed persons, e.g., between "winners" and "losers" in the "global economy." It can build on Lehmann's understanding of conscience-relation as a relation of human claim and

---

9. Bärbel von Wartenberg-Potter, *We Will Not Hang Our Harps on the Willows: Engagement and Spirituality* (Geneva: WCC Publications), 31.

human response, and the agency of conscience in a ministry of humanization.

Conscientizing Encounters

The focus of this book is a dialectical process of recovering and discovering critical faith knowledge that can promote critical faith redevelopment. This involves integrating structural analysis and theological reflection, through conscientization and spiritual discernment. But the larger task is the exploration of the potential of Christian pastoral agency/theology, for empowering liberative and transformative *resistance* to socially constructed dehumanization. This involves acts of ministry congruent with a Christian faith tradition that affirms creation as good. It means speaking of covenant, grace, and *new* creation.

Microcosms of dehumanization, like Gail's "neighborhood," undermine the content of saving knowledge and the adequacy of faith expression. The word of God and the living faith of the dead are seriously compromised in providing meanings that matter to persons assaulted by the hostile facts and spirit of the "global economy." Pastoral theology, as a faith response to "God's unchanging call to heal and care," must attend to human bodies, hearts, and spirits which, like Gail's, are under constant threat of violation and death. This context calls for pastoral theology that develops theory and practice for the ministry of care to both persons who experience harm and those who perpetrate it. "We" need to avoid articulating meanings for "us," in isolation from or at the expense of "them." Pastoral theology needs to facilitate mutually empowering encounters where the faith tradition as covenant, grace, and *new* creation can be critically and creatively tested. The gospel's *uncommon sense* needs to explain itself and make *good sense* to both "winners" and "losers." In "our" own lives, lives in which the *common sense* of the market prevails, it needs to be understood concretely. For many of us, this means integrating the *non-sense* of "losing life to gain it." Such critical faith redevelopment can be experienced as conscientization, through encounter with those who, as survivors of living death or death equivalents, have and can be resources of authentic hope. This may indeed result in life-threatening and life-changing experiences of human connection, from which there is no turning back.

I have argued that a redemptive process of humanization and rehumanization involves dismantling internal supports for denial of harm, through mutual disclosure of the *effects* of harm. This means mutual dialogue, heart-to-heart encounters in which we actively listen to others and critically hear our own voices. Hearing through others' ears and seeing though others' eyes is a critically redeeming faith response to dehumanization as de-emotionalization. We discover, or recover by rediscovery, an original sense of covenant connection, as a real and redeeming alternative to competitive, adversarial relationships. This generates critical faith experience of the actual possibility of humanization. It shows that actual Christians *can* discern the Spirit of a new logic. We *can* be enabled to respond concretely. We *can* experience grace in a world that is not disposed to make a place for it.

Critical faith experience of this covenant connection, in the context of political, economic, and cultural triage, involves rereading. Cover-ups that have obscured biblical options for the weak are removed. The "little ones," valuable as the excluded ones, are discovered, or rediscovered and re-visioned as those who enjoy God's solidarity, *not* as victims, but as recipients of life as a gift from God. Such re-visioning is a risky communal project of critical faith redevelopment.

Potential dialogue partners for a project of mutual disclosure of harm are those in whom human responses can be animated by human claims to personhood. Conscientization is stymied by hardness of heart that is impervious to hearing. Another impediment is anthropological poverty, where there is no basis in conscious experience for making a claim to personhood. Both of these variables are human phenomena in which sinful social structures are manifest. Such prevailing factors make it necessary to recognize the "amazing grace" which enables some voices to speak and some ears to hear. For this reason, I commend mutually empowering dialogue, but only by way of actively *anticipating* grace. Intentional encounter allows for the possibility of discerning and naming channels of grace. The case exemplifies this.

Gail posits a "gooder place." She does so in a moment of grace that is neither praised as "faith" nor explicitly accounted for. Instead, it functions as the point where Edelman apprehends harm. Edelman comprehends and denounces the evil of the "living hell" that robs so many American children of real life. Her critical faith response is one which exhorts and compels participation from others. She precipitates a critical process which rereads Gail's faith claim as a scandal and a challenge. Why does the child need to envision a "gooder place?" By re-visioning America as living up to its promises, Edelman reactivates a faith redevelopment project that insists on making a place for grace, concretely and politically interpreted. This response reveals a source of redemptive knowing. It functions where the virus of dehumanization is detected in triage scenarios such as Newt Gingrich's "Contract With America," or Ontario's "common sense revolution." Out of her faith and life experience, Marian Wright Edelman identifies the antidote. It is contained in "our Old and New Testaments and our American covenant."

At this point, I need to explain my use of and close identification with sources of structural analysis and theological reflection originating in the United States. In such clarification I reveal how case study methodology often involves contextual analysis, and transfer or translation of learnings from the context of the "case" to one's own context. As a Canadian of white, Anglo-Saxon Protestant heritage, I find the ethos of "American manifest destiny" as alienating as that of the "British Empire" and its "white man's burden" to civilize and Christianize the world. Nevertheless, as a Christian, I identify with those Christians and others in the United States who critique the hegemonic posture and economic practice of North American corporatism, both private and public. In a global context, I find it inappropriate and/or impossible to claim a distinct "Canadian" identity. As "Canadians," we cannot distance ourselves from dominant economic enterprises designed to advantage North America. Therefore, I welcome and appropriate the critical analysis of Edelman, Dunning, Rubenstein, Rubin, and others. My choice is reinforced when African and Latin American "partners in mission," such as Omega Bula and Elsa Tamez, acknowledge Canadian particularity. This is because it is precisely in *their* critical analyses that I can recognize my own complicit and privileged economic position as a North American woman who is strategically situated to "win" in the "global economy."

Canadians are indeed subject to the economic power of the United States and may therefore feel "also oppressed." Does this collective experience of diminished national autonomy and economic insecurity foster a sense of identification with the "global economy's" more conspicuous victims? Do we have the self-understanding of those who, in Galeano's words, have always "specialised in losing?" Or, do we claim "legitimate interests" and feel entitled to protect and maximize the competitive advantage of our colonial history and geopolitical position? Do we *live* out of our relationships with those who have specialized in "winning?" Expressed theologically, this is a matter of choice: to accumulate "merits," in good conscience, by maintaining a critical distance between the "saved" and the "damned"; or, to risk shared vulnerability, common struggle, and faith in the justice of God's grace. Tamez addresses the implications of these choices in her reconstruction of the doctrine of justification, from the Latin American Third World perspective. Her examination of justification as an affirmation of life proceeds from two perspectives:

1. justification and the threatened life of the poor, and
2. the gift of being subjects of history as the power of justification by faith.[10]

This informs her understanding of justification as humanization. These are critical perspectives for the task of reconstructing white Canadian Anglo-Saxon good conscience in the context of North American history and identity. They are relevant for the dialogical process commended in this book as a source of conscientization and re-evangelization.

10. Elsa Tamez, *Amnesty of Grace: Justification by Faith from a Latin American Perspective (Nashville: Abingdon Press)*, 121.

I believe that the action of the content of biblical testimony is discernible in the Spirit which Edelman prays will "be born anew *within* and *among* us," in encounters which conscientize, evangelize, justify, and humanize. Resources for informing, animating, and facilitating this critical process are accessible in the analysis and reflection of Canadian theologian Lee Cormie. In "Seeds of Hope in the New World (Dis)Order," Cormie identifies what he considers to be "simultaneously political and religious questions." Complementary to that of Justo Gonzalez, already cited, they set another critical catechetic agenda for the development/redevelopment of faith among Canadian Christians:

> What solidarities, which "others," define me/us?
> What do I/we/others/humanity dare to hope for on this earth?
> What hope can we communicate to our children and to their children?
> Against great odds, how do we ground these hopes?
> How do we join together to make our voices heard in the great debates over the future of the world?
> How do we nurture spiritualities, cultures of resistance and hope in ourselves and our children?
> How do we witness concretely to the Spirit of Life, day in and day out, throughout the stages of our lives?[11]

Reclaiming Real Life for Real Persons

Vicarious dialogue with Marian Wright Edelman, advocate of the "losers" as children "left behind," is a humanizing experience. Critical pastoral dynamics are inherent in her acts of ministry, her proclamation of the faith, her cognate secular knowledge of American history, and her analysis of poverty and racism in America. However, when identified as a resource for the creative work of pastoral theology, I find that much of the *conscientizing* effect of this "case" functions in terms of the personhood of the one carrying out the act

11. Lee Cormie, *Coalitions for Justice: The Story of Canada's Interchurch Coalitions* (Ottawa: Novalis, 1994), 370.

of ministry. It is in the black femaleness of her personhood and her commitment to the "*Black* Community Crusade for Children," which "Gail" makes real and urgent, that Edelman provides concrete pastoral theology. It is such theology which can recover, correct, and expand viewpoints in other branches of theology and ministry.

Toinette Eugene, black woman and ethicist, provides analysis and reflection that informs my identification of these conscientizing factors. Speaking within the framework of her own field of social ethics, she identifies for me the epistemological and hermeneutical significance of race and gender for finding and articulating meanings that matter in a dialogue between "winners" and "losers":

> We know the power of God, and although geography, culture and time are not the same, we also know the universal power of pain and persecution. Pain knows no barriers of time, ethnicity, or gender. . . . The experience of pain can be an occasion, if not a source, of theology and ethics. I wish no pain upon anyone, but its character can afford weighty authority to the voice of the misunderstood, the neglected and abused. The places of this world's pain are nothing less than the geographic centers of "response-able" globalized social ethics. . . .
>
> . . . As a specific vantage point from which to view the broader concerns embedded in social ethics, African and African-American women know a degree of pain that is quadrupled in its intensity. By the time the general pain of human struggle reaches us, it has been passed down from the white man to the white woman to the black man to the black woman — solidified now, fourfold. Frequently, ours is the pain of scar tissue — wounded and "rewounded" in mass brutalization of social, political, economic, and religious strata. Without elevating this woundedness in any way, I do wish to reaffirm that one's way to the universal can only be informed and renewed through an examination of the particulars of one's history and experience, without flinching from what that means, but also with a readiness to use that context for personal and social change. The authority for social change comes from one's own wounds.

Not only has the black woman (and by extension, women of color in general) borne the white world's burdens, she has been a virtuoso burden bearer. Alice Walker observes that generally this woman was the "mule of the world." Her person, her unique spirituality and creativity were suppressed — she never had a "place." . . .

. . . What I am describing here are the primary and deeply painful places where the renewal of moral imagination and solidarity through the expression of a globalization ethics must make itself more adequately and appropriately felt, radically incarnated like a balm in Gilead, in order for globalization to have a more nuanced meaning, in order to make the wounded whole.[12]

In addition to the personhood of the black, female protagonists of God's justice in this "case" study, time and place are hermeneutical factors. The message upon which Edelman's published article is based was delivered in Washington's National Cathedral. This is a church building conceived as a "national" cathedral, to be built and supported by American Episcopalians as a "whole people" and not just as a local parish or regional diocese. The occasion is Martin Luther King Day, a time of commemoration and celebration of a black Christian civil rights leader. One can speculate that her intended hearers are those who remember and value the legacy of Dr. Martin Luther King, Jr. They gather in a ritual that reveals the reality of anti-racist struggle and they acknowledge gains made in enfranchising blacks in America. Yet a hermeneutic of suspicion may condition the hearing of congregants who are aware that the institutionalization of this holiday in 1988, twenty years after King's assassination, was won only through the persistent political pressure of black people and their allies. Such critical hearers know that continuing struggle and black-to-black, white-to-white and black and white dialogue is needed. Only such face-to-face interpretive encounter can facilitate the conversion dynamics that change hearts and minds. Spiritual and ideological change is necessary to overcome backlash and animate proactive energy. Observances that provide adequate expression of meanings that matter, to both blacks and whites, can generate hope and resistance to ongoing polariza-

12. Toinette M. Eugene, "Globalization and Social Ethics: Claiming 'The World in My Eye'!," *Theological Education* 30 (Spring 1993): 10-11.

tion and dehumanization. These sociopolitical and spiritual/theological realities provide interpretive context for Edelman's invoking of Old and New Testaments and the "American covenant." They become biblical and constitutional warrants for claiming real life for all of America's children.

Also functioning to reveal meanings that matter are the intended hearers from whom Edelman anticipates a response on behalf of the forgotten children, made real in "Gail." *Who* and *whose* her hearers/readers are, and whom she believes them to be, can be discerned in the tone and critical content of her proclamatory speech: "Can you and I . . . ? I believe we can. . . . You and I must and can. . . . We are playing politics with human lives." Edelman attributes to those whom she addresses a capacity to hear, care, recognize complicity, and act decisively. This privileges their/our image as human beings. What is it that she knows about them/us, and on what basis?

A response to Edelman's message as the content of saving knowledge derived from the word of God, may function as a critical experience of enhanced being. Her hearers can appropriate the prospect of authentic existence in the redeeming encounter of being reclaimed and affirmed as real. In their personal and collective identities they can "get a life."

Edelman articulates theology by making "Gail" present, as the face, feelings, and suffering of "shameful numbers." She is proclaiming the word of God on an occasion of remembering Martin Luther King, Jr. His blow for freedom initiated a situation of liberation. Homiletically, Edelman actualizes the continuum of this situation of liberation by making a concrete connection between King's "dream" and Gail's "gooder place." She anticipates the possibility for the Spirit's conversion dynamics to make room for grace. In this case, space is created in which persons, both white and of color, can recognize themselves. They can reread and re-vision others, present or absent, living or dead, as reflecting the human face of God. This is a faith-redeveloping process of theological affirmative action. Such affirmation of real life for real persons, through the actual faith of actual people, illumines what James Cone means (cited earlier by Jon Michael Spencer) by revelation as God's self-disclosure to human persons in a situation of liberation.

"I Was Not Scared"

The redemptive knowing that animates Edelman reflects the cumulative tradition of the spirituals, represented by Spencer as
"theological reflection of a long-standing practice of liberation."
The "songs of revelation and liberation" are discernible in her
pastoral action of proclamation and reclamation because that action
is grounded in the historical context of blows for freedom.

In Gail's expression of first-order faith experience, one can
feel the child's apprehension of harm in "a lot of shooting." One
can also discern her comprehension of harm in "really really bad
things." Gail appears to integrate this harm, "I was not scared,"
and to allow for grace by anticipating "a gooder place." Perhaps
the dehumanizing context in which she lives has not yet reduced
her to the anthropological poverty of which Mveng speaks. She is
still able, on the basis of her own experience, to identify and affirm
"some good things in my neighborhood," when it is "peaceful and
quiet and there is no shooting." Or, as one of the next generation
of "virtuoso burden-bearers," she is also a virtuoso hope-bearer.

"I was not scared" can be heard to function as a tentative
opening motif for what Edelman proposes as a third movement for
the "unfinished symphony of justice and opportunity" in America.
As a diminishing echo of "We Shall Overcome," "I was not scared"
is a haunting variation on that performative theme of the second
movement. As a "song of revelation and liberation" it is off-key.
This heightens what is at stake in Edelman's prophetic warning
that "God's unchanging call to heal and care" has never been more
urgent. For me, *hearing* the litany "I was not scared," repeated like
a confession/denial of fear, by a black girl-child at risk, is like *seeing*
Styron's shadow of the thundercloud of the "matter of surplus
population."[13] For this reason, I find that this "case" provides a
means by which I can convey the critical experiential reality of no
room for grace in the contemporary context of "globalization."

Gail is a survivor of death equivalents, i.e., one who has seen
death, been touched by it and lived: "I was not scared." Her survival
makes hope a theological imperative. However, the fragmentation
of her socioeconomic, political, and ideological context is humanly

constructed. The "abundant life" for which she is destined as a child of God, requires that Gail's demonstrated human resilience *not* be confused with Christian hope. It is a child's brave accommodation to experienced necessity. This can be a moment of grace if it inspires fear within and among Christians. We are fearful lest surrogates of hope serve to justify continuing dehumanization as harmless or survivable, and therefore tolerable.

Grace as Critical Appeal

In my perception, it is Marian Edelman who functions as a channel of costly grace. Her redemptive knowing leads her not to exploit Gail's faith testimony, but to discern in it the *presence* of a life-affirming Spirit. This presence functions to actualize in Edelman, and make recognizable to others, the theology of Elsa Tamez. Tamez articulates her encounter with and experience of the human face of God, in the context of Latin America. Edelman calls forth the Spirit, "to be born anew" as an animating force for the reclamation of children. A faith claim cited earlier from Elsa Tamez provides a sound theological rationale for this invocation:

> When the solidarity of the Triune God — as friend and as brother or sister — is received by faith, this presence of God through the Spirit turns into a permanent critical appeal to conscience in the paths of justice.

Edelman denounces decisively the forces that cause Gail to envision a "gooder place" as one imaginable only *beyond* her own neighborhood. Edelman announces her own faith that "you and I" can join in a counter-triage reclamation project to "Leave No Child Behind." Saving content informs such a ministry of humanization, as human response to human claims to personhood. Edelman's concrete critical faith in the solidarity of God, and what she expects because of it, actualizes the presence of the Spirit.

13. Richard L. Rubenstein, *The Cunning of History: The Holocaust and the American Future* (New York: Harper and Row, 1978), xi.

Conscientization as Re-evangelization

Being Born Again as Truly Human

The actual time and actual place of Edelman's act of ministry, the narrative and rhetorical setting, the encounter between saving content, living faith, and escalating dehumanization are dialectical ingredients of a critical theological process. They make it possible to recognize such a process as "conscientization" and "re-evangelization." These terms can be appropriated from Willem Saayman's re-visioning of the context of South Africa:

> Re-evangelisation implies . . . a process of *conscientization,* of becoming aware and of making others aware of the injustice and oppression caused by a system which often prided itself on being 'Christian,' and of the good news that God in Jesus totally rejects such injustice and oppression; . . . implies *empowerment,* the courage to be fully human, to overcome the inhumanity of being either oppressor or oppressed; . . . implies *liberation,* the freedom to be fully human, demonstrated for example in the exodus events and in the life death and resurrection of Jesus of Nazareth. . . . I think one can best deal with this subject by differentiating between the re-evangelisation of the White church, that of the Black church, and that of the patriarchal church.[14]

In order for Gail, as a survivor of death equivalents to experience real life, Edelman's hearers must be re-evangelized. There must be a concrete faith response to the rehumanizing project she envisions. This involves dismantling denial mechanisms and reconstructing good conscience through mutual disclosure of harm. False and authentic spirits, which nourish fear and hope in counterfeit and genuine forms, need to be discerned and tested. For Christians, this can happen concretely and communally. As "winners" and "losers" in the "global economy," we can empower each other as partners equal to the task of personal and structural analysis. In

14. Willem Saayman, *Christian Mission in South Africa* (Pretoria: University of South Africa, 1991), 108-9.

Saayman's context, this is a daunting task in which a process of unlearning and relearning is required to rehumanize persons dehumanized by the apartheid system:

> White South Africans need to be made aware how the centuries of oppression of Black South Africans has led not only to the dehumanisation of Black people, but also to the dehumanisation of Whites. To create, in the course of three centuries, a sophisticated, but totally soulless system such as the system of apartheid, to define and treat human beings simply as units of labour, to refuse to share in Christian fellowship with other human beings . . . cannot but warp extensively what is left of one's humanity. White South Africans need to be made aware of this serious shortcoming. But it is only Black South Africans who can actually lead them along the way to recover their humanity, for it is a (for the Whites) new humanity they have to recover; their *African* humanity.[15]

Rehumanization calls for conversion dynamics that function to unmask and denounce false images and announce liberation from them, in *concrete* terms. The depth of dehumanization which has to be overcome, and the scope of conversion required, in terms of the concrete rehumanization which is needed, is evident in a Cox News Service item from Johannesburg, South Africa. The item was published by the *Halifax Chronicle-Herald* as part of a special feature on the Fourth World Conference on Women, in Beijing:

> Ask a black woman in South Africa if she knows anyone who has died "at home, alone and smelly." It is likely she will, says Dr. Sharon Fonn, because cervical cancer is the leading cancer killer of poor women in the country and across Africa. The cancer typically spreads to the bowels or bladder, leading to what Fonn describes as a "humiliating, lonely death" in which the incontinent patient is shunned because caring for her is too unpleasant. But cervical cancer is also among the most detectable cancers and among the easiest to stop. . . . Cervical

15. Ibid., 110.

cancer is a disease which sets off the disparity between the apartheid-era health care that has been available for South Africa's impoverished black majority and that provided for its white minority who were the focus of medical spending. . . . The Pap test . . . costs about $11 in South Africa and could be made widely available, unlike in other African countries where medical care is far less organized. But it has never been a consistent part of the public health procedures because, Fonn said, in white-ruled South Africa there was never the political will to supervise health care for everyone.[16]

To me it is ironic but ominous, that the efforts of some to deinstitutionalize such political triage in South Africa, in the wake of liberation from apartheid, coincides with the zeal of others to introduce elements of triage into the public health systems of "developed" societies of the "democratic" West. This alarming phenomenon underlines the significance of Saayman's call for the church's ministry of care to be a *missio politica oecumenica*, i.e., a ministry of humanization by persons who have recovered their "new humanity" as members of a global humanity. James Dunning describes the redemptive, revelatory dynamics that can impel a conscientizing process of concrete re-evangelization:

> Any approach in conversion which purports to offer healing in the real world seriously betrays the Gospel if it does not confront these demons which oppose the reign of God. . . . Goodness is more than us. . . . Healing comes . . . not through the language of guilt or despair nor rage nor cheap grace but through the language of grief and compassion and also hope which releases the genuine power of people created in God's image.[17]

Sölle designates our social existence as the place for testing the truth of affirmations that creation is good. She also describes how and why this testing must be done with self-critical rigor. More

16. "Viewpoint," *Halifax Chronicle-Herald* (Sept. 2, 1995).
17. James Dunning, "Confronting the Demons: The Social Dimensions of Conversion," in *Conversion and the Catechumenate*, ed. Robert Duggan (New York: Paulist Press, 1984), 26.

than twenty years ago, in *Political Theology*, Sölle addressed a phenomenon of ideological captivity engendered by capitalism, and the
inadequacy of Christian responses to it:

> It is not enough to criticize property rights and the import duty
> imposed on manufactured goods from developed countries, so
> long as we, as "powerless" individuals, are not able to clarify
> how we are entangled in the general structures and how we
> conform to the introverted norms that we regard as self-evident
> — for example, the norms of achievement, consumerism, reasons
> of state — and pass them on to others, even when we reject them
> privately and verbally.[18]

As a redemptive, dialogical process undertaken in community, testing truth claims involves the critical faith dynamics of repentance,
in response to recognition of sin. This involves apprehension and
comprehension of harm. Harm is named by those who experience
its reality and yet believe that through grace, new sight and hence
re-visioning is possible. For Sölle (as later, for Tamez) this process
necessitated overcoming the inadequacies of traditional theological
language regarding the forgiveness of sin. The possibility of "non-
social forgiveness" (i.e., forgiveness and conversion linked solely
to God as absolute Lord) was inconceivable according to Sölle's
understanding of sin as social/political, and "forgiveness, politically
interpreted," because:

> To experience the forgiveness of sins, we need a group of human
> beings who make it possible for us to begin afresh; at the very
> least we need partners who accept us as we are, who have faith
> in our repentance, who believe we are capable of conversion.[19]

Her convictions as to the crucial connection between communal,
corporate faith experience and "world-transforming praxis" are
reflected in the following statement made at that time:

18. Dorothee Sölle, *Political Theology* (Philadelphia: Fortress Press, 1974),
92.
19. Ibid., 104.

The difficult and the future task of political theology consists in speaking appropriately of the gospel. . . . what is involved is giving credibility to the possibility of liberation from oppressive structures; what is involved is the inducement-model for becoming truly human. Thus, so it appears to me, theological theory offers less help than the strengthening of faith experienced in the present-day *communio sanctorum*. . . . The letter of Christ that we ourselves are is further received and read. There is no other letter capable of replacing the letter of Christ that we are.[20]

Sölle's redemptive knowing is borne out in the "case" of Edelman's conscientizing project. It can be recognized as an inducement-model for being human. Edelman herself actualizes the letter of Christ that can be received and read in a conversion process of communal re-evangelization. Such a process of humanization may be implied in what Rubenstein calls for as a religious transformation, a call to conversion, to be "born again as men and women blessed with the capacity to care for each other here and now."

For Christians, as "winners" and "losers" in the "global economy," being born again as truly human means living as a *new* creation, whose goodness is tested in the experience of a global humanity. This new creation will prove to be a "gooder place" than "the living hell" of their current existence, when children of a global humanity are protected from the virus of triage which infects them with expendability. Protection is dependent upon their credentials, as real persons, made in the image of God. If such theological credentials are to qualify real persons for real life and not living death, they must pass the test of market forces which can render them null and void. Engaging those forces becomes the agenda for critical pastoral praxis in which conscientization and re-evangelization facilitate justification as concrete humanization. This begins as a project of redeveloping faith in the possibility of a good creation, as the "gooder place" of a rehumanized *oecumene.*

20. Ibid., 107.

Living Between Fear and Hope

Edelman prays for the presence of the Spirit *within* and *among* us. This invokes a dynamic critical agency that cannot be fixed individually, conceived of narrowly, or prescribed definitively as "hope." It's a liberative dynamic of anticipation as hope in action that characterizes Edelman's ministry of humanization. She is animated by the reality of fear in the lives of American children. The hope that she prays will be actively and discernibly *within* and *among* us is a hope which is connected to that fear, yet not paralyzed by it. This is fear that can be experienced as grace, if and when it teaches hearts and minds to see anew. Those who experience dis-grace, yet in their fear are "not scared," can mediate relief from fear. They are channels of grace, not because they *have* hope, but because they make room for grace in a world bent on squeezing it out. "I have some good things in my neighborhood."

Appendix One

Excerpts from the "To Be a Woman: African Women's Response to
the Economic Crisis" Video Resource Guide

Produced by the Interchurch Coalition on Africa
for
The All Africa Conference of Churches — Women's Desk

Writing: Njoki Kipusi, Karen Ridd
Editing: Omega Bula, John Mihevc
Nairobi, Kenya, 1992

Introduction

This guide was created in order to help facilitate audiences of the
video as they work to deepen their understanding of Structural
Adjustment Programmes (SAPS) and their effects on African economies. The video was produced for African women participating in
workshops on economic literacy. It is also for those who wish to
gain a better understanding of SAPS, their impact and to learn about
the struggles, strategies and coping mechanisms of African women.

Economic literacy is an essential element in women's lives. It
creates awareness not only of what seems obvious, but of what

otherwise might have been dismissed as of no consequence. The introduction of SAPS that was meant to restructure the lives of people in Third World countries, has become a global concern. This should make every individual responsible for creating awareness of the specificity of economic issues as experience on a day-to-day basis as well as on a global level. This process might then create a human dimension to the various economic policies and programs!

History of Third World Debt

1. 1970s — oil prices rise, causing an excess of capital in northern banks: banks looking for borrowers, "Third World" countries looking for development dollars.
2. 1980s — interest rates sky-rocket, loans become mathematically impossible to pay back, "Third World" countries pay back debts, many times over in their interest payments, the South subsidizes the North on a scale of 3 to 1.
3. In order to "help" debtor countries pay back, IMF and World Bank provide "fresh" loans on the condition that debtor countries adopt Structural Adjustment Programmes (SAPS).

International Monetary Fund

1. Established in 1946 to create a stable system of exchange rates and an open international trading system.
2. The IMF voting system is not based on a one country one vote system. Rather, voting is done according to the amount of money that each country has paid into the Fund.
3. The IMF lends money to countries experiencing balance of payments problems in return for changes in domestic economic policies.
4. IMF loans were considered to be needed only as a short-term remedy to address temporary problems. However, since 1986 the IMF has taken out of Africa over $4 billion more than it has put in.

The World Bank

1. Created in 1946, originally to finance the reconstruction of war-torn Europe. In the 1950s it began to turn its attention to developing countries to finance medium and long-term development by providing loans for projects.
2. As a result of the debt crisis, the World Bank has also changed to provide Structural Adjustment Loans, in coordination with the IMF, to countries who cannot meet their balance of payments. New loans to indebted countries are now provided only if the country agrees to both IMF and World Bank conditions.
3. Voting power is like that of the IMF, according to the share of the contribution.

Explaining Structural Adjustment Programmes (SAPS)

SAPS stands for Structural Adjustment Programmes. This is the name given to all the conditions the IMF and the World Bank attach to loans given to debtor countries. What are the policies of a SAP?

- Severe cuts in spending on Social Services like Health and Education
- The removal of subsidies on food, etc.
- Currency devaluation (this makes imported goods much more expensive and exported goods much cheaper)
- The promotion of exports to raise foreign exchange
- Trade liberalization (Foreign goods enter the country without a duty and foreign companies are allowed to compete with local companies)

Appendix Two

Thirty-fifth General Council of the United Church of Canada
August 1994

Excerpts from the Report of the Moderator's Task Group
on Canada's Economic Crisis

PART ONE
The World as It Now Is
(because we have chosen to see it
and act in it that way)

Preamble:

"Crisis" is a pale word to describe our time. For the majority of
the earth's people "holocaust" is nearer their daily reality. Such a
world is a denial of God. Many, perhaps most, are losing hope. This
is just as much the case in the affluent world as in the hungry one.
A narrowed and abstracted theory of economics rules the household. The people worship idols. God weeps.

We live in a world with extreme gaps of poverty and affluence.
Our economic systems are structured in our imaginations and our
institutions to maintain and broaden gaps. This is an affront to God.

PART TWO
The World as God has Created It
(because we have chosen to see it
and act in it this way)

Preamble:

The practice of justice, love and peace in a disfigured, terrorized world is no easy matter. But we do not live as those who have no hope. In our unjust world we long for, and live for, the kin-dom of God, where all are responsible for all. Animated by this vision, we hold that these embodiments of the kin-dom show it near: life lived according to the common good; global security with other humans; ecological solidarity; the preferential option for the poor; labour over capital. The world belongs to God.

PART THREE
An Invitation to Seed Planting

Preamble:

The economic crisis which is the central issue of our church and our society is a profoundly spiritual one, as we have sought to indicate above. All who are Christians, and can imagine the world as God does, are called to faith/action. All at General Council are "co-missioners," first to the Council and then, more importantly, to the world. The mission of all of us, ecumenically, is to announce and bring to pass the good news of "salvation" — which is to say, healing. We are inhabited by God's Spirit, not to condemn the world by the way we live, but that the world through us might be saved.

So the church is called to act for change, and on, we suggest, three levels: (1) of the life of each individual member; (2) of the life of the church itself in its structures and performances; (3) of the life of the world as a whole, particularly in naming and deconstructing the structures of sin that bind "the house" in death.

Permissions

Sidney E. Ahlstrom, *A Religious History of the American People.* Copyright 1972 by Yale University. Permission to quote granted by Yale University Press.

Patrick Bond, "Bell Curve Tolls for Africa." Permission to quote granted by *African Agenda.*

Jonathan Bonk, "Globalization and Mission Education." Permission to quote granted by *Theological Education.*

"Concerned Evangelicals," *Evangelical Witness in South Africa: A Critique of Evangelical Theology and Practice by South African Evangelicals.* Permission to quote granted by Wm. B. Eerdmans Publishing Company.

Lee Cormie, *Coalitions for Justice: The Story of Canada's Interchurch Coalitions.* Permission to quote granted by Novalis.

David Crane, *The Canadian Dictionary of Business/Economics.* Copyright 1993 by David Crane. Part of this book originally appeared in *A Dictionary of Canadian Economics* published by Hurtig Publishers Ltd. in 1980. Selection reprinted by permission from Stoddart Publishing Co. Ltd.

Ulrich Duchrow, *Europe in the World System 1492-1992: Is Justice Possible? Copyright 1992 WCC Publications, World Council of Churches, Geneva, Switzerland.*

Marian Wright Edelman, "An Unfinished Symphony: God's Unchanging Call to Heal and Care." Reprinted with permission

152

Englebert Mveng, "Third World Theology — What Theology? What World?: Evaluation by an African Delegate." From *Irruption of the Third World: Challenge to Theology*, ed. Virginia Fabella and Sergio Torres. Permission to quote granted by Orbis Books.

Mercy Oduyoye, "Contextualization as a Dynamic in Theological Education." Permission to quote granted by *Theological Education*.

Jaroslav Pelikan, *The Christian Tradition*. Copyright 1971 by the University of Chicago. Permission to quote granted by the University of Chicago.

John Pobee, *Research Report 16: The Worship of the Free Market and the Death of the Poor*. Permission to quote granted by Life and Peace Institute.

Richard L. Rubenstein, *The Age of Triage: Fear and Hope in an Overcrowded World*. Copyright 1983 by Richard L. Rubenstein. Reprinted by permission of Beacon Press, Boston.

Lillian B. Rubin, *Worlds of Pain: Life in the Working-Class Family*. Copyright 1976 by Lillian Breslow Rubin. Permission to quote granted by HarperCollins Publishers, Inc.

Willem Saayman, *Christian Mission in South Africa*. Permission to quote granted by Willem Saayman.

Wilfred Cantwell Smith, *The Meaning and End of Religion*. Permission to quote granted by Augsburg Fortress Publishers.

Dorothee Sölle, *Thinking About God: An Introduction to Theology*. Permission to quote granted by Trinity International, Philadelphia.

Jon Michael Spencer, *Protest and Praise: Sacred Music of Black Religion*. Reprinted by permission of Jon Michael Spencer, copyright 1990 by Augsburg Fortress.

John G. Stackhouse, Jr. "Billy Graham and the Nature of Conversion: A Paradigm Case." Permission to quote granted by *Studies in Religion/Sciences Religieuses*.

John Stackhouse, "Putting a Head Count on Poverty." Reprinted with permission from *The Globe and Mail*, Toronto.

Elsa Tamez, *The Amnesty of Grace: Justification by Faith from a Latin American Perspective*. Permission to quote granted by Departamento Ecumenico De Investigaciones, Costa Rica.

Index

Ahlstrom, Sydney: British in the New World, 82; confidence of Christopher Columbus, 71-72; creating a new past, 58

Barlow, Maude, 34-35
Barrett, David, 88
Bonhoeffer, Dietrich, 129-30
Bonk, Jonathan, 14
Bula, Omega, 12-13, 134

Columbus, Christopher, 69, 71-72, 77
"Concerned Evangelicals," 64
Conscience: as social construct, 25, 103; "good conscience" ("Christian Conscience"), 29, 74, 87, 89, 101-2, 112, 116, 134, 142; liberation of, 125
Conscientization: 102, 128, 130-32, 135, 136; as re-evangelization, 141-46
Consciousness: critical, 6, 18, 24, 29, 45, 55, 74, 90, 101, 108, 126; false (uncritical), 41, 56, 68, 101, 103
Conversion: critical, 13, 15, 100,

143-45; dynamics of, 99, 119-20, 138, 142
Cormie, Lee 135
Czerny, Michael, and James Swift, 90

Dehumanization, x-xi; examples, 26-29, 116, 124, 125, 130-33, 140-43; origins, 56, 142; threat to pastoral theology, 15-16, 18, 113-16, 119, 120; working definition, 5
Derber, Charles: hard triage, 39; surplus population, 38
D'Escoto, Miguel, 63
Dis-grace, ix, 76, 89, 146
Duchrow, Ulrich, 77-78
Dunning, James, 143-44

Economics: theologically interpreted, 10-11, 16. *See also* Globalization; and Global economy
Edelman, Marian Wright: analysis of dehumanization, 124; as channal of grace, 140; introduction of, 123
Eugene, Toinette M.: black women's experience, 136-37,

156

www.ingramcontent.com/pod-product-compliance
Lightning Source LLC
Chambersburg PA
CBHW071100280326
41928CB00050B/2576